AF421797

BELONGING OVER INFLUENCE

How Brands Earn Cultural Residency

MARLINO BITANGA

Belonging Over Influence: *How Brands Earn Cultural Residency*

Copyright © 2026 Marlino Bitanga

Published by Makeeta, LLC. www.makeeta.co

The moral right of the author has been asserted.

For quantity sales, speaking inquiries, or media enquiries, please contact the author at the website address above.

Library of Congress Control Number: 2026913369

ISBN:
979-8-9962557-0-2 (hardcover)
979-8-9962557-1-9 (paperback)
979-8-9962557-2-6 (ebook)
979-8-9962557-3-3 (audiobook)

All rights reserved. No part of this book may be reproduced, stored in a retrieval system, or transmitted in any form or by any means, electronic, mechanical, photocopying, recording, or otherwise, without the prior written permission of the author. All inquiries should be directed to the author at the website address above.

Disclaimer: Although the author has made every effort to ensure the information in this book was correct at press time, the author does not assume and hereby disclaims any liability to any party for any loss, damage, or disruption caused by errors or omissions, whether such errors or omissions result from negligence, accident, or any other cause.

FIRST EDITION

To God, my Lord and Savior for the frequency.

*To my wife and our kids, who are the
community I am most proud to belong to.*

*To my parents, who understood what
Rizal proved long before I did.*

*To my cousin, whose garage in 1989 was
the first room where I felt it.*

*To the community that built the world this
book is about, long before anyone thought
to write it down.*

And to Filipino music, which was always the proof.

**Ang hindi marunong lumingon
sa pinanggalingan ay hindi
makararating sa paroroonan.**

*He who does not look back at where he came
from will not reach his destination.*

— Filipino proverb

CONTENT

The Flag-Washing Trap

—

I should tell you something I rarely tell anyone in professional settings. For most of my career in marketing, creative and brand strategy, I hid the fact that I was a DJ. Not because I was ashamed of it. Because I had worked hard to be taken seriously in rooms where DJs were entertainment, not strategists, and I didn't want the two identities to cancel each other out. So I kept them separate. The DJ on one side. The marketer on the other. A firewall between them that I maintained for years.

Writing this book made me realize that firewall was a lie I told myself. The DJ was never separate from the strategist. It was the foundation of the strategist. Reading the room, feeling the energy, knowing what to play and when, building belonging in real time with music as the tool. That is the same skill set. I just applied it in two different rooms.

In 1999, I attended F.I.N.D., the Filipino Intercollegiate Networking Dialogue. I was there because I was building a Filipino magazine called ISA. Not a lifestyle magazine in the traditional sense. An urban magazine focused on documenting the Filipino culture that nobody else was covering. The DJs, the artists, the dance crews, the Filipino cheerleaders at professional sports teams. The community that was building something real and loud and entirely its own, outside of the nursing schools and the engineering programs and every other lane the mainstream expected Filipinos to occupy.

At that conference I heard Kiwi and Faith Santilla for the first time. A Filipino MC rapping with full authority. A Filipino voice doing spoken word that stopped the room. I had never heard anything like it. Not because it was technically impressive, though it was. Because it was completely, unapologetically Filipino in a form I loved, and it didn't ask anyone's permission to exist that way.

That same weekend I watched *José Rizal*, the film co-produced and directed by Marilou Diaz-Abaya, written by Jun Lana, Ricky Lee, and Peter Ong Lim. The story of the Filipino national hero imprisoned under Spanish colonization, told through the final days before his execution. I sat in that screening and something shifted permanently. I understood, in a way I never had before, why my parents pushed so hard for education. Why being a nurse, a doctor, an engineer, a professional in a high-paying field mattered so deeply to the generation that came before mine. It wasn't about status. It was about what Rizal proved: that knowledge is the one thing no colonizer can take from you. That empowerment through understanding is the most durable form of freedom there is.

I walked out of that screening a different person than I walked in.

Every time I have leveled up since then, from DJ to radio to marketing to brand strategy to the book you are holding right now, I have asked myself the same question: what can I do now that uses everything I have learned up to this point? I never left anything behind. The DJ informed the marketer. The marketer informed the strategist. The Filipino informed all of it. They were never separate. I just spent years pretending they were.

This book is what happens when you stop pretending.

I was standing in a boardroom with the creative team of a major professional sports franchise. Outside the stadium walls, the city held one of the largest Filipino populations in the country. Families who had lived and breathed that team for generations, who had worn the colors through championships and losing streaks alike, who had made that stadium part of their identity long before anyone in that room thought to acknowledge it. We were there to design the giveaway item for their Filipino Heritage Night.

I laid my proposal on the table.

It wasn't just a hat. I had replaced the team's primary colors with a palette pulled from the textures of Tinikling plaid, not as a costume, but as a conversation. And across the front, instead of the team name, I chose a single word in Tagalog: *PANALO*. Win.

I explained what that word was doing there. To a casual observer passing through the gift shop, it was just a cool design, something different, something that stood out. But to a Filipino resident sitting in those stands, seeing their language on their team's gear, untranslated and un-captioned, was a completely different kind of moment. It wasn't just acknowledgment. It was declaration. It said: you belong here, and we already know what that word means because we're one of you.

The room went quiet in the way rooms go quiet when something makes people uncomfortable. Then the corporate safety kicked in.

The creative team recoiled. Tagalog was "too risky." The general audience wouldn't understand it. They asked to put the primary hex codes back. They suggested replacing *Panalo* with "Filipino Heritage Night" in a standard corporate font, the kind of font that exists on every heritage night promotion for every demographic in every city in America. And then came the line that told me everything I needed to know about where this was going:

"Can we just fill our logo with the colors of the Philippine flag?"

That's what I now call *flag-washing*. The flag is the loudest, most surface-level symbol available. It requires zero research, zero nuance, and zero real relationship with the community it's meant to honor. It's the move you make when you want the optics of inclusion without the vulnerability of actual understanding. By choosing the flag over the language, they were telling the Filipino community something they'd never say out loud: our brand guidelines matter more than your identity.

I looked at the final version, a generic hat with a flag stuffed into a logo, and it felt like exactly what it was. Extraction dressed up as representation. Here's the part I don't usually tell: I approved it. I pushed back, I made my case, and when it was clear the room wasn't moving, I signed off on the compromise. I told myself it was a first step. That you have to get in the room before you can change the room. That something was better than nothing. The hat went out. It didn't sell, not poorly, not "room for improvement," it genuinely didn't move. The Filipino families we were supposedly celebrating looked at it and kept walking, and they didn't need to explain why. The empty box said it for them.

I already knew why. I knew it the moment I approved it.

When you remove the soul from something to make it safe, you don't end up with a safer version of the original idea. You end up with no idea at all. *Panalo* would have cost them nothing and said everything. And I let them take it off the hat because I thought half a step forward was better than standing still. That experience taught me something I've never forgotten: compromise in cultural work isn't a middle ground. It's a message. And the message that hat sent was that the community was worth a flag but not worth a word.

That moment is where this book starts, not with the right answer, but with the wrong one, and what it cost.

I've spent over two decades watching this same collision play out across boardrooms, partnerships, sponsorship decks, and Heritage Nights in cities across the country. On one side are the organizations obsessed with the numbers, brands trying to sell a culture the way you'd sell a billboard, renting the aesthetic for a quarter and calling it community engagement. On the other side is the world I've lived in as a DJ and a creator: the energy that happens when a community actually feels recognized, when the signal is right, when the room knows you were paying attention long before you needed something from them.

Those two sides don't naturally find each other. That's the gap this book is trying to close.

In 2007, I launched a podcast I'd been building in my head since 2006, a simulated local hip-hop radio station playing only music by Filipino hip-hop and R&B artists. At the time, I had nineteen independent artists in rotation. When I revived it in 2019, that number had grown to over 350, an entire generation of Filipino artists who had developed their craft, built their audiences, and created a body of work that was world-class by any standard. The talent had arrived. What hadn't arrived was the corporate infrastructure to recognize it, support it, or build with it intentionally.

That gap still exists. And it exists not because the culture is niche, it was never niche, but because the organizations with the budgets and the platforms have been looking at Filipino culture the way that boardroom looked at my hat. They see a flag. They don't see the word.

There is a concept at the heart of Filipino culture that explains why this matters more than most brands understand. It is called *Kapwa*, the core Filipino value of shared identity, of seeing yourself in others and others in yourself, of treating every person you encounter not as a stranger but as someone in whom your own humanity is reflected. *Kapwa* is not a marketing concept. It is a centuries-old way of moving through the world. It is why the community responds the way it does to every Filipino athlete, artist, and creator who steps onto a major platform, not just with pride, but with ownership, as if the achievement belongs to everyone who shares that identity. Because in the *Kapwa* framework, it does.

Understanding *Kapwa* is the key to understanding why belonging, for this community, is not a nice-to-have. It is the operating system. When a brand earns genuine belonging with a *Kapwa*-driven community, it doesn't just acquire customers. It becomes part of something the community carries forward on its own, because the community sees itself in what the brand has built. And when a brand fails to earn it, when it flag-washes, when it extracts, when it shows up as a tourist, the community doesn't just disengage. It remembers. *Kapwa* runs in both directions.

Most brands right now are running on what I call the execution treadmill: chasing influencer metrics, buying reach, optimizing for impressions, and wondering why the results keep getting thinner. The model they're running was built entirely on visibility, the idea that if you can get in front of enough people with the right message often enough, you can manufacture desire.

Culture doesn't move on visibility. It moves on belonging. And belonging doesn't scale the way brands are used to. It doesn't spike and flatten on a campaign timeline. It compounds. It builds through presence and consistency and cultural fluency, through being in the room before you need something from the room. You don't earn it with a one-off post or a Heritage Night hat. You earn it by showing up in a way that makes the community feel like you actually understand the world they've built.

That's the shift this book is about.

Influence fades because it was always rented. Trust stays because it was earned. And in a world where audiences have developed a near-perfect radar for the difference between a brand that belongs and a brand that's just passing through, trust is the only currency that still actually converts.

If it belongs, it doesn't need to persuade. If it still needs to persuade, it doesn't belong yet.

The Filipino community is not a niche. It never was. It's a case study in what belonging actually looks like when it's built right, and a clear warning of what happens when it isn't.

Let's start with what's been going wrong.

Influence was built to move people. It was never built to become part of where they live.

THE LIMITS OF INFLUENCE

The marketing world has been running on the same promise for decades: buy enough attention, wrap it in the right message, repeat it often enough, and you can manufacture desire. The entire industry was built on that premise. Platforms were engineered around it. Careers were built defending it. And for a long time, it worked well enough that nobody asked too many questions about what it was actually costing. That era is ending, and the receipts are starting to show up everywhere.

What we're living through right now isn't just a shift in consumer behavior or a new wrinkle in the algorithm. It's something more fundamental: a correction. For years, brands operated like tourists in culture, renting moments they didn't earn, flying in creators to perform authenticity for a camera, treating block parties and desert festivals

They just had to show up speaking a language their community already lived in, and the community did the rest.

The brands watching that same festival are starting to feel the same gap from the other side. Brands are now quietly ghosting the very influencers they spent the last decade fighting over, not because the budgets disappeared, but because the trust did. Ten thousand perfectly curated posts created a sea of sameness that audiences learned to tune out, and the brands that paid for all of it are left holding reach metrics that no longer translate into anything real. They bought visibility. They never bought entry.

The era of broadcast is giving way to something different: an era of residency, where the room only listens to the people who actually live there. Brute force, scale, and frequency were always tools for reaching people from the outside. They were never designed to build the kind of trust that makes a community carry your brand forward on their own. In a world defined by deep cultural signals and communities that can spot a tourist from a mile away, that distinction is no longer a nuance. It's the whole game.

Earned belonging. That's what's missing. And you can't buy your way to it.

CHAPTER 1

The Illusion Of Influence

—

For the better part of a decade, the marketing industry has been measuring the wrong thing. In every boardroom, every strategy deck, every quarterly review, influence has been treated as the definitive proof of growth, the number that ends the argument and justifies the spend. Reach enough people, deliver a sharp enough message, repeat it with enough frequency, and behavior will follow.

The problem is that exposure and alignment are not the same thing, and the gap between them is where the whole model starts to fall apart.

It is entirely possible, and increasingly common, for a brand to reach millions of people and still fail to connect with a single one of them on a level that actually matters. The message lands, the impression is counted, the dashboard turns green, and the community that was supposedly being reached looks at the whole thing and keeps scrolling. Not out of indifference. Out of recognition. They know exactly what they're looking at, and they've decided it isn't for them.

The "Oob" Paradox

I remember the morning the ube rollout hit my feeds.

I was scrolling through my Filipino Facebook groups and Tik-Tok, and the reaction wasn't what a brand marketing team would have hoped for. There was no "we made it" energy, no celebration that a major global chain had finally discovered something from our culture. What I saw instead was a collective wince, people calling out the mispronunciations multiplying across social media, pointing at the neon-violet syrup clearly designed for the grid rather than the palate, and telling each other to skip the drive-through and go to an actual Filipino bakery if they wanted to know what ube really tasted like.

A global brand had looked at Filipino culture, found a color palette they liked, and lifted it cleanly away from the hundred-year story it belonged to, the Aeta harvesters, the family kitchens, the birthday cakes and halaya and everything that made ube ube before it became a Spring Trend. They treated a cultural staple like a Pantone swatch. That's what extraction feels like from the inside. Not anger, exactly, more like the specific exhaustion of watching something that belongs to you get hollowed out and repackaged for someone else's aesthetic moment, while the people who kept it alive for generations don't even get a mention in the press release.

And the thing is, it didn't have to go that way. If I were architecting that rollout, the first thing I'd have done is lead with the pronunciation, a simple, genuine campaign: it's oo-beh, not oob, taught by Filipino creators and Lolas who've been saying it correctly their whole lives. That's not a correction. That's an invitation. It tells the community that the brand did the work, that they understand they're guests in this story, not the authors of it.

I'd have built a Roots Initiative alongside the product launch, use the platform to point people toward local Filipino-owned bakeries, the ones that have been making halaya and ube cake for decades. A global chain doesn't need to compete with those businesses. It can be the on-ramp that leads people to them. That's what belonging-first strategy actually looks like in practice.

Instead, the brand chose scale and lost the soul. And when that happens, the community doesn't thank you for the representation, because what you delivered wasn't representation. It was decoration.

The Limits of Reach

What that ube moment illustrates is something that's become increasingly true across the board: audiences have developed a near-perfect marketing radar. They recognize the patterns. They know when something is designed to move them toward a purchase rather than speak to who they are, and the moment that intent becomes visible, the default response is to disengage, not passively, but actively. They aren't just ignoring the ad. They're rejecting the intrusion, and sometimes they're doing it publicly in ways that cost the brand far more than the campaign was ever worth.

This doesn't mean influence is dead. In the right context, it still works exactly as designed. When the decision is transactional, a commodity purchase, a low-stakes choice that doesn't require any deeper alignment with identity, influence can move the needle efficiently. It's a perfectly functional tool for shallow water.

But transactions aren't culture, and the moment you step into a cultural environment, where heritage lives, where identity is at stake, where the community has a long memory and a sharp eye for what's authentic, the rules change completely. People stop evaluating the product and start evaluating you. They're asking whether you fit within the world they've built, and that evaluation happens faster than any piece of marketing copy can reach them. If the accent is wrong, if the timing is off, if something about the whole thing feels like a tourist who read about the neighborhood instead of someone who actually lives there, it creates a friction that no amount of reach can fix.

The Insider Loophole

Here's a pattern I've watched play out more times than I can count. A global brand decides they want to show up authentically in a cultural space. They put real money behind it, high production, the right guest list, an event that looks, on paper, like genuine engagement. And sometimes it actually works, at least on the surface. The photos are good. The community shows up. The internal team calls it a win.

But if you look closely at how it actually happened, you'll usually find one person who made it possible, a single cultural advocate inside the organization, someone from the community who used their personal relationships to pull the brand into spaces it hadn't earned its way into. One person who knew the right people, understood the right signals, and quietly translated the brand into something the community could accept.

That's not cultural residency. That's a really good local guide.

And the proof is in what happens when that person leaves. When they move on to a different company or a different role, the brand's connection to that community evaporates with them, because the connection was never actually the brand's. It was theirs. The organization never built the process, the genuine understanding, or the long-term relationships that would have made the work sustainable. They borrowed someone's belonging and called it their own.

If your cultural relevance lives in a single person rather than in the way your organization actually operates, you are still a tourist. A well-connected one, but a tourist nonetheless.

The fundamental limitation of the influence model is the direction it runs. It moves from the outside in, it assumes that behavior can be shaped through external pressure, that audiences are targets to be reached rather than environments to be understood. That assumption works fine when the goal is a transaction. It fails completely when the goal is genuine integration into a world that already exists and already has its own standards for who belongs there.

Influence was built to move people. It was never built to become part of where they live.

That's what we're really talking about when we talk about belonging, not a softer version of influence, not a more authentic-sounding campaign strategy, but a fundamentally different model for how brands enter and earn their place in cultural environments. One that starts not with what you want to say, but with whether you've done enough to deserve a seat in the room at all.

The Word the Industry Doesn't Have

Most marketing frameworks don't have a word for what they're actually missing. They can describe reach, frequency, conversion, engagement, sentiment. They can measure impressions and optimize for clicks. But they don't have language for the thing that makes a community carry a brand forward on its own, unprompted, without a campaign pushing them. They call it "authenticity" when they're trying to name it from the outside. They call it "loyalty" when they're trying to measure it. Neither word gets close.

Filipino culture has the word. It has had it for centuries.

The word is *Kapwa*.

Kapwa is the core value at the center of Filipino psychology, the concept that Filipino scholar Dr. Virgilio Enriquez spent his life articulating and that generations of Filipinos have carried without needing to name it, because it was simply the way they moved through the world. In English, the closest translation is shared identity, but that doesn't fully capture it either. Professor Elizabeth Protacio De Castro, who spent her career at the University of the Philippines Department of Psychology, puts it this way: *Kapwa* in English is I, you, and we together in one word.

Not I. Not you. Not even we as a group of separate individuals. The self and the other, held in the same word, because in the *Kapwa* worldview they are not actually separate to begin with.

The Filipino language encodes this at the grammatical level. Consider *Mahal kita*, the Filipino expression for I love you. In English, the subject is explicit: I. I love you. The I is the anchor of the sentence, the individual self doing the loving. In Tagalog, the subject I disappears entirely. *Mahal* means love. *Kita* means you and me together. The self is not just de-emphasized. It is dissolved into the relationship. The grammar itself says: there is no I that exists independently of the you.

That is *Kapwa*. Not as a cultural nicety, not as a value statement on a nonprofit's website, but as the structural logic of how identity is understood and expressed. The self is always already in relation to others. Your belonging is constitutive of mine. When something good happens to a Filipino on a world stage, the community doesn't just feel proud on their behalf. They feel it as something that happened to them, because in the *Kapwa* framework, it did.

This is why the ube rollout failed at a deeper level than the mispronunciation. It treated Filipino culture as an external object to be borrowed, a color palette to lift, a trend to capitalize on. But *Kapwa* means the community was never just observing the rollout from outside. They were inside it, experiencing it as something being done to something that was theirs, that was them. The extraction was personal because in a *Kapwa*-driven community, culture is never impersonal.

You belong, or you don't. And the community has always known which one you are before you've finished your pitch.

CHAPTER 2

Why People Don't Want To Be Convinced

—

Something fundamental has shifted in the relationship between brands and the people they're trying to reach, and it has nothing to do with attention spans or platform algorithms. It has to do with knowledge.

The era of information asymmetry is over. The average person scrolling their feed today has absorbed more marketing than any previous generation in history, not as a student, not intentionally, just by existing in the world. They know what a paid partnership looks like before they see the disclosure tag. They can feel the structure of a six-week campaign flight in the way content is paced. They recognize the hollow cadence of corporate damage control within the first sentence of the statement. They have, whether they asked for it or not, developed a PhD in how this industry works. And that knowledge has permanently changed the physics of persuasion.

In high-context cultural spaces especially, people have stopped asking does this make sense and started asking something harder: does this fit. Those are two completely different questions, and only one of them can be answered with better copy.

The Ghost at the Table

I've been to GoodPhil and Friendship Games, two of the largest student-run Filipino-American events in the country, the kind of gatherings where over seven thousand NextGen students come together for days of competition, performance, and the specific, irreplaceable energy of a community that has built something entirely on its own terms. I've watched what happens when brands show up to those spaces, and the range of what I've seen tells you almost everything you need to know about why the influence model breaks down in cultural environments.

At one of these events, a legacy food brand, a household name, something that has genuinely been in Filipino pantries for decades, had paid for a sponsorship. They had a banner. They had a table. The table was unmanned. Not for a few minutes while someone grabbed lunch, but for the duration. A banner flapping in the background of a space that was absolutely electric with community energy, and nobody from the brand there to do anything with it.

To the marketing team that signed off on the sponsorship, this probably looked like a line item successfully executed. Presence at a major cultural event, brand visibility, reach. But to every student who walked past that empty table, it sent a signal that no amount of media spend can unsend: we paid for the ticket but we didn't care enough to show up. The brand wasn't seen as a supporter. It was seen as a tourist who bought the pass and stayed at the hotel. In a space built entirely on participation and collective labor, that absence wasn't neutral. It was a statement.

The Parent at the Function

At another event in the same circuit, a different brand tried harder and still missed, in a way that was almost more instructive than the empty table.

They had staff on the floor. They had a real presence. But the staff were dressed in stiff corporate polos and black slacks, standing behind their table in a room full of students who were there to celebrate their identity, their music, and each other. The brand stuck out the way a chaperone sticks out at a school dance, not unwelcome exactly, but unmistakably out of place. And the brand, despite physically being present, was communicating through every visual signal available, the clothes, the posture, the setup, that it didn't understand the world it had walked into. It was trying to speak the language of business in a room that was conducting an entirely different conversation. Presence without proximity isn't belonging. It's observation with a budget.

The Persistence of Friction

When brands run into this kind of resistance, the industry-standard response is to optimize. Refine the message. A/B test the creative. Tighten the targeting. Turn up the volume and try again. And every one of those responses makes the problem worse, because they're all built on the same flawed assumption: that the issue is the quality of the signal rather than the fundamental misalignment between the brand and the environment it's trying to enter.

If you don't fit the context, a stronger message doesn't fix the gap. It widens it. It makes the intrusion more visible, not less. The community doesn't respond to increased volume with increased openness. They respond with increased resistance, because now it's clear that the brand isn't listening, it's just talking louder.

From Persuasion to Infrastructure

The question that changes everything isn't what message will move these people. It's does this brand have an earned place in this environment at all.

That's an operator-level question, and most marketing teams aren't set up to ask it because the answer requires a kind of honesty that quarterly planning cycles don't reward. It requires admitting that you might not belong yet, that the work of earning a real place in a cultural community is slower and less legible than a campaign flight, that it can't be compressed into a Heritage Month activation or a single well-intentioned sponsorship.

But here's what's true on the other side of that honesty: when something genuinely fits, when a brand has done the work, built the relationships, contributed to the environment in ways that actually matter to the people inside it, the need for persuasion disappears entirely. Nobody has to be convinced. Engagement becomes the natural response, the path of least resistance, because the brand has stopped being something that's happening to the community and started being something the community recognizes as part of its own world.

That's the shift. Not from bad marketing to good marketing, but from persuasion to infrastructure. From trying to move people toward you, to building something worth moving toward.

CHAPTER 3

When Influence Works, And Why It's Weak

—

Let me be clear about something before we go any further: influence hasn't stopped working. To say otherwise would be intellectually dishonest, and it would also make everything else in this book easier to dismiss. Influence still moves needles. In the right context, it moves them efficiently. The point isn't that the model is broken everywhere. It's that most brands are deploying it in places where it was never designed to work, and then wondering why the results keep disappointing them.

Understanding exactly when influence works is just as important as understanding when it doesn't, because the ceiling of one is the floor of the other. Know where influence runs out of road and you'll know precisely when you need to switch models.

Influence is most effective in low-context environments, situations where the stakes are low, the decision is straightforward, and identity isn't really part of the equation. You need paper towels. You're choosing between two streaming services. You're picking a hotel for a business trip. In these moments, the relationship between brand and audience is transactional by nature, and transactional relationships respond well to influence. There's no expectation of long-term connection, no deeper evaluation of whether the brand fits within the world you've built for yourself. There's just a decision to be made, and a well-placed message can make it.

The moment the context shifts from utility to identity, the moment a person is evaluating not just what something does but what it says about who they are, the effectiveness of influence drops off a cliff. And in cultural environments, that shift is not the exception. It's the entire terrain.

The Categorization Trap

I first ran into the structural limits of the influence model in the mid-to-late nineties, working in and around radio. This was the era when artists like Jocelyn Enriquez and groups like Pinay, One Voice, and Innerlude were breaking into mainstream rotation, Filipino artists making world-class Hip-Hop and R&B that could stand next to anything on the charts. I watched them get traction and then watched the industry quietly let them fall out of rotation, and at some point I asked a record rep directly why it was so hard for Filipino artists to hold onto that mainstream presence once they'd earned it.

His answer stayed with me: "We don't know how to market Filipino artists. We don't know how to categorize their sound."

That was the influence model revealing its own limitation out loud. The industry's entire infrastructure for breaking artists was built around pre-packaged categories, buckets that determined which radio format got the pitch, which retail section got the placement, which demographic got the targeted ad spend. Filipino artists didn't fit cleanly into any of the existing buckets, and rather than build a new one, the industry treated them as anomalies and moved on. The music was undeniable. The system just didn't have a slot for it.

Decades later, the same *Corporate Excuse Framework* is still running. The diaspora is "too niche." There isn't enough data. The audience is hard to reach. Meanwhile, in the lead-up to Coachella 2026, the search term BINI Coachella hit a perfect interest score of 100 on Google Trends, the second most-searched act on the entire festival lineup, behind only Justin Bieber. When they took the Mojave Stage as the first Filipino group from the Philippines to perform at Coachella, the community was already there waiting for them.

The data was never missing. The system just wasn't built to see it.

The Identity Barrier

In environments where identity is the stakes, a perfectly persuasive message that doesn't align with who someone is will always stay outside the door. It doesn't matter how well-crafted it is, how precisely targeted, or how many times it's served. If it doesn't fit the world the audience inhabits, it doesn't get in.

This is why the most culturally resonant Filipino-American artists aren't treating their heritage as a marketing strategy. They're treating it as a frequency. When H.E.R. played Belle in the live-action *Beauty and the Beast*, she called the costume designer personally and asked to do something important to her Filipino culture. The result was an apron featuring hand-painted Baybayin script, the ancient pre-colonial alphabet of the Philippines, spelling Belle in the writing system that Spanish colonization nearly erased. She didn't explain it in an interview. She didn't caption it. She just wore it, and the community that recognized it felt something that no amount of explicit representation could manufacture. Olivia Rodrigo timed the release of her third album to June 12, 2026, Philippine Independence Day, while building her promotional rollout around Filipino cooking content and global karaoke pop-ups. Neither of these were marketing beats in the traditional sense. They were high-context signals, the kind that influence models don't know how to value because they only measure what everyone can see.

The same logic is showing up in Hollywood through what I've started calling the *Zero Caption* phenomenon. In *Spider-Man: No Way Home*, there's a scene where Ned and his Lola speak to each other entirely in Tagalog, no subtitles, no explanation, no translation for the general audience. *The Cleaning Lady*, *The Pitt*, *St. Denis Medical*: the same choice, made deliberately. In the old influence model, you translate everything. You make it accessible to the broadest possible audience because reach is the metric. In the belonging model, you leave the captions off. The message to the resident is immediate and unmistakable: this moment is for you, and we trusted you to find it. For everyone else, it's a signal that they're guests in someone else's house, which is, in itself, a form of respect that communities notice and remember.

The Certification Moment

There is a specific kind of institutional event that gets mistaken for cultural discovery, and the Super Bowl halftime show is the clearest example of it at the largest possible scale.

When Bad Bunny performed at the 2026 Super Bowl, the show was extraordinary. Entirely in Spanish, no translation offered. Sugar cane fields on the stage. The specific iconography of Puerto Rican and Latino culture rendered at full resolution, the cameos, the symbols, the sounds, all of it deployed without apology or explanation. Cardi B, Karol G, Jessica Alba: none of it announced, all of it immediately legible to the community that had been building toward this moment for years.

But the NFL did not discover Latino culture that night. The halftime show does not discover culture. It certifies culture that has already reached critical mass, culture that has been moving through communities, sustaining itself through its own energy for years before any institution decides it's safe enough to put on a stage watched by a hundred million people. The certification moment is not the beginning of the story. It is the institutional acknowledgment that the story has been running long enough that ignoring it is no longer an option.

That gap, between when culture actually arrives and when institutions finally acknowledge it, is where the influence model bleeds out most visibly. Influence is supposed to move culture forward. At the institutional level, it almost always moves behind it, ratifying what the community has already built rather than helping build it.

I've been watching this gap play out in Filipino culture for over thirty years. The pattern is consistent across every name, every moment, every art form: the community carries the culture, builds the ecosystem, sustains the momentum, and then, years later, the institution shows up and frames it as a discovery.

BINI at Coachella may be our certification moment, the point at which the institution could no longer look away. And now I'm hearing what I've been waiting to hear: brands are calling. There's genuine interest in Filipino artists that didn't exist in boardroom conversations not long ago. SB19 is making their debut at Lollapalooza. The certification is happening.

But every brand currently picking up the phone needs to understand one thing: the community was here before you called. What you're experiencing as a discovery is what the community has been living inside for decades. If you show up now with the same outside-in logic that made you late in the first place, treating this as a trend to capitalize on rather than a residency to earn, the community will recognize exactly what you are.

A tourist who arrived after the party started and is trying to take credit for the music.

The certification moment is an invitation. What you do with it determines whether you ever actually belong.

The Operational Nightmare

Here's where the weakness of influence becomes not just a strategic problem but a financial one. Influence can generate attention. It cannot guarantee acceptance. It can create movement, but it cannot create residency, the kind of sustained, self-reinforcing presence that keeps a brand relevant in a cultural environment long after the campaign has ended.

The reason is structural. Influence is an external force. It's applied to an audience from the outside in an attempt to change their behavior, and it works for exactly as long as the pressure is maintained. The moment the media spend stops, the movement stops. There's nothing left inside the environment to hold the brand in place, because the brand never actually integrated into the environment. It was always just pushing against it.

I've watched this play out across budget cycles more times than I can count. A brand invests heavily in a cultural moment, gets the visibility metrics they were looking for, lets the campaign flight end, and then wonders six months later why the community doesn't seem to remember they were there. They weren't there, not really. They were pushing from outside the window. And when they stopped pushing, the community simply closed the curtain and moved on. This isn't a creative failure. The work is often genuinely good. It's a model failure. Influence was designed to initiate action, not sustain it. It was built for transactions, not relationships. And in the cultural environments where the most valuable, most loyal, most community-driven audiences live, transactions are the lowest possible form of connection.

The ceiling of influence is the moment identity enters the room. Past that point, you need something else entirely, a model built not on external pressure but on genuine integration, on earning a place inside the environment rather than trying to push your way in from outside it.

ILLOCOS NORTE
LTFRB CASE NO. 2001-04528
ILLOCOS NORTE
ILLOCOS NORTE
GOD BLESS OUR TRIP
YH·804
General
drugstore

THE JEEPNEY LOGIC

*How a repurposed vehicle
became a philosophy*

To truly understand the difference between influence and belonging, you have to look at how people move.

The Western transit model is built on control. There is a fixed route, a centralized authority that determines the schedule, the stops, and the destination. The passenger's role in this system is entirely passive. You wait at the designated point, you pay the fare, and you are delivered to a predetermined location. If the bus doesn't stop where you are, or doesn't go where you need to be, that's your problem. You are an outlier. The system does not bend for you; you bend for the system. Success is measured by efficiency, adherence to the plan, and how closely the actual route matches the intended one.

That's the influence model in physical form.

In the Philippines, the Jeepney operates on a completely different logic, and if you've never ridden one, no description fully does it justice, but let me try.

The Jeepney has a general route, but it has no fixed stops. It moves through the world in a state of constant, fluid negotiation with the people who inhabit it. To get on, you don't look for a sign or wait at a marked location. You signal to the driver from wherever you happen to be standing, and the vehicle comes to you. To get off, you don't wait for a bell or a recorded announcement. You knock on the roof, or you make a specific sound, *para*, or *para po* if you're being polite, and the environment stops for you. The route exists, but the route serves the people, not the other way around.

What makes the Jeepney a masterpiece isn't just its flexibility. It's the participation it requires from everyone inside it. Because the vehicle is almost always crowded, paying your fare isn't a transaction between you and a machine. It's a collective act. You hand your money to the person next to you. They pass it to the person next to them. It moves hand to hand down the length of the vehicle until it reaches the driver, and the change makes its way back through the same human chain. No one is a passive passenger. Everyone has a role. The journey survives because every person inside it is actively contributing to its survival.

The bus is a campaign. The Jeepney is a system.

The bus requires constant infrastructure and top-down control to function. If passengers stop following the rules, the whole thing breaks down. The Jeepney thrives precisely because it doesn't rely on rigid rules. It relies on the collective intelligence of everyone moving through it together. It doesn't try to impose order on the road. It reads the road as it actually is, congested, unpredictable, communal, and moves accordingly.

When a brand operates like a bus, it builds designated stops and then wonders why the community isn't waiting at them. It designs a fixed route and then gets frustrated when culture doesn't travel in straight lines. It mistakes its own infrastructure for relevance, and then spends more money trying to get people to stand where it wants them to stand, rather than asking where they're actually trying to go.

When a brand operates with Jeepney Logic, it stops building stops and starts reading signals. It understands that its value isn't in the route it controls but in the environment it creates, an environment where people have real roles, where the journey is genuinely shared, where the brand moves because the community moves and survives because it has given everyone inside it something meaningful to contribute.

It's about how you move with them.

The bus is a campaign.
The Jeepney is a system.

*Culture doesn't move
on visibility. It moves
on belonging.*

WHAT BELONGING DOES INSTEAD

The autopsy is done. We've looked at the influence model from enough angles to understand not just where it fails, but why. It's a system built on brute force and volume that works perfectly until it doesn't, and the moment it steps into a room where identity and community set the terms of engagement, it has nothing left to offer. It can buy a transactional spike. It can manufacture a moment of visibility. But it cannot buy its way into a world that has its own language, its own rituals, and its own very clear sense of who belongs there and who is just passing through.

So the question changes.

We stop asking how to persuade an audience and start asking something harder: how do you inhabit a world that isn't yours yet? How do you earn a place in an environment that was built without you, that functions perfectly well without you, and that has seen enough tourists to know one on sight?

Belonging operates on a different set of physics entirely. It doesn't run on psychological hooks or repetitive reach or the sheer force of a media budget. It runs on alignment, on how seamlessly you fit within a world that already exists, on whether your presence adds something real to the environment or just adds noise.

This is not about finding better marketing. It's about installing a different operating system, shifting from being the intruder trying to steal thirty seconds of attention to being the resident that the neighborhood would actually miss if you left.

It starts with the fastest, most unforgiving reflex in all of human culture. Recognition.

CHAPTER 4

Belonging Feels Different

The difference between influence and belonging isn't theoretical, and you won't find it in a creative brief or an analytics dashboard. You find it in your body. It's the split-second instinct that tells you, before your brain has finished processing, whether you're being welcomed into something real or being sold a version of it.

When a brand operates through influence, every interaction is a negotiation, a request for a loan of someone's time, and the interest rates are brutal. The moment a message hits a screen, the audience's defenses engage automatically. Who is this? What do they want from me? Is this worth the next thirty seconds of my life? Even the most beautifully produced, perfectly targeted piece of content has to clear that hurdle before it can do anything else. Belonging doesn't have to clear that hurdle, because the hurdle isn't there.

The Evaluator vs. The Resident

Think about the difference between a stranger knocking on your door at nine o'clock at night and a family member walking into your kitchen. The stranger triggers something in you, a wariness, a need to assess, a decision about whether to open the door at all. The family member is just a continuation of your day. One requires an explanation. The other is an assumption. The energy required is completely different, and no amount of the stranger being polite or well-dressed or holding something that smells good changes the fundamental dynamic.

That's the mechanical reality of what belonging does that influence can't replicate. When something fits, genuinely fits, not as the result of careful targeting but because it was built from inside the world it's entering, the evaluation step disappears. The community doesn't need to decide whether to let it in. It's already home.

This is the deeper logic behind the Zero Caption phenomenon I mentioned earlier. When a creator removes the subtitles, they're not just making a stylistic choice about accessibility. They're making a psychological decision about who the work is centered on. By refusing to translate, they remove the friction for the resident and, in doing so, trigger an immediate recognition reflex. The audience doesn't have to evaluate what they're watching because they already recognize where they are. The brain responds to home differently than it responds to an ad. And that difference is everything.

It changes the physics of how work moves through a community. In a belonging-driven model, you're not fighting for a seat at the table. You're already on the guest list. You're not disrupting a conversation; you're contributing to one that's been running for years without you. That's why a fifty-thousand-dollar community-led project can move through a culture with more velocity and genuine heart than a ten-million-dollar campaign. The campaign has to buy its way past the friction at every step. The community project is already part of the flow.

The Jo Koy Frequency

If you want to see these physics demonstrated at the largest possible scale, look at what happened on March 21, 2026, when Jo Koy and Gabriel "Fluffy" Iglesias sold out SoFi Stadium in Los Angeles for the first-ever stand-up comedy show at the venue.

To anyone operating inside the traditional influence model, that number is a mathematical impossibility for what the industry still quietly calls "ethnic" comedy. The logic has always been that specificity is a niche, and niche doesn't fill stadiums. To reach seventy thousand people, you're supposed to sand down the edges, broaden the appeal, make it accessible enough that nobody feels excluded, which in practice means making it generic enough that nobody feels particularly seen either.

Jo Koy did the opposite. His work is unapologetically, specifically Filipino, not as a disclaimer or a cultural footnote, but as the entire foundation. The nursing expectations, the Santo Niño on the dashboard, the specific weight of an immigrant mother's silence when she's disappointed in you. He doesn't reference the Filipino experience; he builds entire worlds out of it and invites you to live inside them.

Netflix originally passed on his first special, *Live from Seattle*. Didn't see the vision. So Jo Koy didn't wait for their permission. He self-funded the whole production, paid for the cameras and the venue and the crew out of his own pocket, and bet his life savings on the belief that what the gatekeepers were calling a niche was actually a universal pulse. When he finally sold that special to Netflix, it didn't just perform. It shattered the algorithm, because the algorithm wasn't built to predict what happens when a community that has never been properly centered finally sees itself reflected at full resolution.

What Jo Koy demonstrated is what I call *Lateral Alignment*, the phenomenon where being deeply, specifically true to one community creates a frequency that adjacent communities can also feel. His Filipino-specific material didn't exclude the Latino audience in that stadium. It acted as a mirror. They weren't laughing at someone else's family; they were recognizing their own. Specificity, done with real depth and real love, doesn't narrow the audience. It deepens the resonance for everyone in the room.

But here's the part of the Jo Koy story that the industry still hasn't fully absorbed: the moment the gatekeepers got involved and started optimizing, the frequency broke. When Hollywood took his life and ran it through the standard studio formula, *Easter Sunday*, complete with car chases and loan sharks and every generic trope designed to make a "cultural" film feel safe for a general audience, it traded the specific, high-context rhythms of a Filipino kitchen for the kind of broad accessibility that ends up being specific to no one. The film tried to explain the community to tourists instead of speaking to residents, and in doing so lost the exact gravity that fills stadiums. *Easter Sunday* barely cleared thirteen million dollars in its entire theatrical run. The math is not subtle.

Even someone with Jo Koy's genuine cultural credibility loses the frequency the moment he stops aligning with the room and starts optimizing for the gatekeeper. That's how powerful the distinction is. This isn't about talent. It's about the direction the work is facing.

The Heavy Rotation Inverse

I built Heavy Rotation because I needed proof that this shift in physics was real and reproducible, not just a theory I was carrying around from years on the floor.

In the corporate music world, "heavy rotation" is a status you buy or earn through data and volume. It means the gatekeepers have decided your work is worth repeating. I wanted to flip that entirely. I wanted to build a world where a Filipino artist, someone the industry had decided didn't fit any of its existing categories, could hear the words you're on Heavy Rotation and feel what those words were supposed to mean, not just that their music was being played, but that it was being valued. That the work mattered. That there was a world that recognized it.

Over an eight-year stretch, from 2017 through 2025, artists of Filipino heritage dominated the major Grammy categories: Kalani Pe'a, H.E.R., Olivia Rodrigo, Bruno Mars, Steve Lacy, Jesse Barrera, and Jeff Bernat. The scale the industry keeps saying doesn't exist is literally at the top of the charts. But the giants keep missing it because they're measuring influence metrics while these artists are building belonging kingdoms. They're looking for the data that confirms what they already understand, and the culture is busy doing something the data wasn't designed to capture.

Alignment vs. Optimization

The influence model solves for friction through optimization, sharper copy, louder visuals, more precise targeting, a smoother path to the conversion. The goal is to make the pitch so seamless that the audience doesn't notice they're being pitched. It's a fundamentally defensive strategy, built around the assumption that the audience's default is resistance and the brand's job is to overcome it.

The belonging model solves for friction through alignment.

You don't adjust the work after the fact to make it more palatable. You build it to fit the environment from the beginning, which means doing the work of understanding that environment before you build anything at all. The friction doesn't need to be overcome because it was never created in the first place.

Influence-driven work is a burst, a spike in visibility that exists for exactly as long as the media spend supports it and disappears the moment it doesn't. If you have to keep paying for people to notice you, you haven't built a relationship. You've rented a billboard.

Belonging-driven work becomes residency. You know it's working not when the campaign metrics look good, but when the work is circulating in private group chats six months after the flight ended, when it has become part of the community's daily rituals, when it's so woven into the fabric of the environment that people would notice if it were gone. That's what it means to be part of the cultural furniture rather than a poster on the wall.

The first pillar of how belonging is actually built is the one that happens fastest and matters most: Recognition.

CHAPTER 5

Recognition: It Has To Feel Like Life

—

Belonging begins with a reflex. Not a decision, not an evaluation, not a carefully considered response to a well-crafted message, a reflex. Before a person decides to engage with anything, before they've consciously processed what they're looking at, something faster and more fundamental has already rendered a verdict. It happens in the gut, not the brain. And what it's assessing, in that fraction of a second, is whether what they're seeing feels like life or feels like a set.

That's Recognition. And it's the first thing belonging requires.

Representation is a Checklist. Recognition is a Pulse.

The reason Recognition is so rarely achieved in brand work is that it gets consistently confused with something easier and less demanding: Representation. Representation is about the who, the presence of the right faces, the right demographic checkboxes, the visible markers of inclusion that signal to a community that they've been accounted for in the casting brief. It matters. But it's the floor, not the ceiling, and too many brands mistake reaching the floor for the whole job.

Recognition is about the how. It's not whether the faces are there. It's whether the world those faces inhabit feels true. It's the difference between a Filipino family appearing in a campaign and a Filipino family that moves, speaks, eats, and exists in the specific, unrepeatable way that Filipino families actually do. One is a checklist item. The other is a pulse.

There's an episode of *All American: Homecoming*, "Godspeed," that demonstrates this distinction more clearly than any brand campaign I've seen in years. Netta Walker, who is Blasian in real life, plays a character named Keisha who is honoring her late Filipino mother on what would have been her birthday. Her friends at Bringston University don't throw a generic memorial gathering with vaguely multicultural food and well-meaning platitudes. They execute a *Kamayan* feast, the traditional Filipino communal meal where food is laid out on banana leaves and eaten with your hands, together, without the mediation of plates or utensils or any of the formality that creates distance between people and their food and each other.

They didn't just put Filipino food on a table and call it representation. They covered the surface in banana leaves. They served crispy pata, fried fish, fried squid, and buko pandan with fresh coconut drinks. They ate with their hands. The non-Filipino characters didn't show up in whatever they happened to be wearing. Peyton Alex Smith, who plays Damon, wore a *Barong Tagalog*, and Keisha and Dr. P wore modern embroidered boleros, because that's what the moment called for and they understood that without being told. Nobody explained why. Nobody narrated the cultural significance for the benefit of viewers who might not know. The scene simply assumed the residency of the culture, treated it as the self-evident reality it is, and let the community in the audience experience the specific, irreplaceable feeling of seeing their world rendered accurately.

The Parol Standard

Disney UK's 2020 Christmas short "*Lola*" demonstrates the same principle at a completely different scale, and what makes it worth studying isn't just what's in the film. It's who made it.

Angela Affinita, Director of Brand Marketing and Creative for Disney EMEA, drew directly from her own Filipina grandmother's tradition of making *parols* when she developed the campaign. Her quote says everything: "Being able to draw on my own experience with my Filipina grandmother and the making of star lanterns to bring a level of authentic creativity is pretty special." The film that resulted wasn't a brand team's interpretation of Filipino Christmas culture. It was a resident's memory rendered in animation, and the community could feel the difference immediately.

The three-minute short centers on a grandmother and her granddaughter living in the UK, bonding over the yearly tradition of making a *parol*, the traditional Philippine star-shaped lantern that symbolizes the Star of Bethlehem and has been a centerpiece of Filipino Christmas for centuries. The *mano*, the gesture of respect to elders, appears without explanation. The *parol*-making ritual unfolds without a caption. Filipino Christmas starting in the *Ber* months, September through December, is assumed rather than explained. None of it is subtitled for a global audience. The film simply builds a story around these specifics and trusts the audience to either live inside it or, if they're outside it, to feel the warmth of something they may not fully understand but can clearly feel.

The community's reaction was immediate and overwhelming. Disney EMEA's highest-performing Facebook post ever. Over 106 million views on that film alone. Filipinos across the diaspora described it with the same word, not represented, but seen. Those are different things, and the distance between them is exactly what this chapter is about.

I know because I felt it myself. I watched that film for the first time alone, and by the end of it I was somewhere else entirely. I was back in my lola's kitchen. She was the one who took care of us when my parents were both at work, the one who cooked for us, watched over us, held the house together in the specific quiet way that lolas do. What came back wasn't a single memory. It was a feeling, the conversations we used to have about the Philippines, about living in America, about cooking, about love, about all the things she understood without needing to explain them. The film didn't remind me of her. It returned me to her. That's not what representation does. That's what recognition does.

Disney returned with "*The Stepdad*" in 2021, following a now-grown Nicole as her family welcomes stepdad Mike, whose Jamaican heritage is woven into the film alongside the continuing Filipino cultural thread. *Parols* appear throughout, Lola's original *parol*-making kit is visible in the background, and Nicole's dining area is lined with traditional Filipino decorative wooden objects. The sequel didn't dilute the Filipino cultural foundation to accommodate new cultural representation. It built on top of it. By 2022 the campaign had become a trilogy, with both the 2020 and 2021 films reaching over 184 million combined views.

The follow-up tutorial Disney released on how to make a *parol* is worth noting separately. The tutorial is for tourists. The films were for residents. Disney understood the difference and kept those two things in their appropriate order. The recognition came first, uncompromised. The invitation to learn followed. That sequencing is the whole lesson.

The Shorthand of the Resident

Recognition lives in the shorthand, the details that are invisible to the outsider but immediately, unmistakably present to the resident. And what made that *All American* scene land with the weight it did wasn't just the banana leaves or the crispy pata or the *Barongs*. It was something the audience could feel without being able to name.

The photographs used in Keisha's memorial scene were real photographs, actual photos of Netta Walker and her mother. The storyline carried its own deep personal resonance for Netta, who lost her father as a young adult, and what was written as a character's grief became something that lived in a completely different register for the person performing it. She said afterward that her younger self felt loved and seen in a way she never imagined possible.

When the shorthand is that precise, when the accuracy comes not from research but from lived experience, from a creator putting something genuinely personal into the frame, the audience doesn't see a scripted moment. They see a heartbeat. They feel the difference even when they can't articulate it, because authenticity has a texture that craft alone cannot replicate. The resident knows the difference instantly. They always do.

Compare that to the standard brand version of a Filipino family gathering, the stock-photo table, the dishes with names that sound right, the smiling faces that could belong to any campaign for any brand in any market. It's not offensive. It's just empty. It passes the representation checklist and fails the recognition test entirely, because it was assembled from visible markers rather than built from the inside out. The checklist is satisfied. The pulse is absent.

The Litmus Test: The Refusal to Explain

Here's the clearest signal that recognition is present or absent in any piece of work: whether it feels the need to explain itself.

In that *All American* scene, nobody paused to explain why the characters were wearing *Barongs*, or offer a brief cultural history of the *Kamayan* tradition, or subtitle the Tagalog, or make any of the hundred small gestures that signal to an outside audience that the creators are aware not everyone will follow along. The scene simply existed in its own cultural logic and trusted the audience to either live inside that logic or recognize, without resentment, that they were guests in someone else's house.

When recognition is missing, over-explanation rushes in to fill the gap. Brands do this constantly, they include the cultural element and then immediately surround it with context and captions and reassurances, layering explanation on top of representation until the original gesture is buried under the weight of its own justification. And every word of that explanation sends a signal. It tells the resident that the work was built for someone else and adjusted to include them, rather than built for them from the beginning. The tourist narrates their experience of the culture. The resident simply exists within it. Over-explanation is the tell. The refusal to explain is the proof. The resident doesn't need the caption. The resident is the caption.

From the Wall to the Floor

Recognition is the vibe check that gets you through the door.

It's the moment the community looks at what you've made and decides, in that first unrepeatable second, that you were paying attention, that you understand the world you're trying to enter, that you're not a tourist wearing a costume made from someone else's culture. It's necessary. But it's not sufficient.

Because recognition alone is still observational. It's a picture on the wall, accurate, resonant, worth something, but it's still something the community is looking at rather than something they're living inside. The work has passed the test, but passing a test and belonging are not the same thing. You can be recognized without being accounted for. You can be seen without being needed.

The shift from looking to living, from being acknowledged to being part of the action, is what the next pillar is about.

In that *All American* episode, Keisha's friends didn't honor her mother's culture by learning about it and then stepping back to let Keisha grieve alone. They participated in it. They wore the clothes, ate the food, sat at the table, and were present in the specific way that grief and love and community require all at once. They didn't watch Keisha heal. They became part of how she healed. The culture wasn't a backdrop. It was the mechanism.

That shift, from recognition to active, meaningful participation, is where belonging starts to compound.

CHAPTER 6

Participation: No Role, No Belonging

—

Recognition opens the door. Participation determines whether you walk through it and stay.

Once a community has recognized a brand as something that might belong, once the vibe check has been passed and the initial signal has landed correctly, the relationship enters its most critical and most fragile phase. The question now is whether it can actually function inside the environment, whether it can take a role and fill it with something real rather than just occupying space while waiting for the next campaign moment to justify its presence.

Participation is not activity. This is one of the most important distinctions in the entire belonging framework, and it's the one that trips up the most brands. Activity is measurable: posts, events, impressions, engagements. Participation is something else entirely. It's the quality of the involvement, the degree to which what you're doing actually matters to the people you're doing it with, the sense inside the community that you are genuinely part of what's happening rather than running a parallel track alongside it. Activity can be manufactured. Participation has to be earned.

The Difference Between Showing Up and Being There

Most brand activations fail at participation not because the execution is bad but because the role was designed from the outside in. The brand decided in advance what it was going to do in the community, built the activation around that decision, and then entered the space and performed it. The community was cast as the audience. The brand was the star. And the result, no matter how well-produced, feels exactly like what it is: a brand doing something for a community rather than doing something with one.

The test is simple: if the brand disappeared from the activation tomorrow, would the community miss what it provided, or would they barely notice? If the answer is the latter, the brand was never really participating. It was performing.

GoodPhil and the Architecture of the Room

The clearest example I've seen of participation done right, at least in the context of Filipino cultural events, is what happened at GoodPhil. I was there throughout the event, DJing. The night opened with JMKO, a Filipino artist who warmed the room the way only a resident can, not by performing for the crowd but by performing with them, using the kind of familiar cultural shorthand that tells the audience they're in safe hands before the first hook lands. By the time AJ Rafael headlined, the room wasn't an audience anymore. It was a community that had been building energy together for hours.

At one point I dropped *"Clarity"* by Zedd, a deliberately non-Filipino record in a deeply Filipino room. The choice wasn't random. It was a read. A specific moment in the room's arc where the energy needed to peak before it could settle into something deeper. The record worked not because Zedd is Filipino but because I understood where the room was and what it needed in that moment. That's the difference between a DJ who programs a set and a DJ who reads a room. One is executing a plan. The other is participating.

That's the standard. Not: what did we plan to do here? But: what does this room actually need, and can we provide it in a way that makes the environment better rather than just louder?

One Band, One Sound: Friendship Games

There is a version of participation that doesn't require a brand to build anything. It requires a brand to recognize something that was already built and show up inside it with enough honesty to let the environment do what it was always going to do.

Friendship Games began in 1986 at California State University Fullerton, started by CSUF's Pilipinx American Student Association. By the time I encountered it during my early radio years, it had grown into the largest student-run Pilipinx American event in the nation, over forty Filipino American student organizations from college campuses across California, Nevada, and Arizona, gathering for a day of competitive games, performances, and what they call S.P.U.F.: Spirit, Pride, Unity, and Friendship. The school that shows the most S.P.U.F. wins an eight-foot trophy. Nobody is being paid to be there. Nobody needs to be told what to do. The whole thing runs on a forty-year-old tradition that students carry forward because it belongs to them.

I found out about Friendship Games through friends at Bay Area schools who were making the trip down to Fullerton. I knew immediately that the station needed to be there. None of our competitors were going to show up. They didn't know this world existed or didn't think it was worth the trip. I went to my program director at Wild 94.9 in San Francisco and told him directly: we need to be at this event, these are our people, and we should be in that room. He approved it, covered the flight and accommodations, and sent me down.

When I got on stage and did a live on-air call-in, it was my very first live call-in as a radio DJ. I didn't fully know what I was stepping into. What happened next was something I wasn't fully prepared for. Over ten thousand students started chanting, their schools, their Filipino clubs, their organizations, all at once, overlapping and building on each other until the whole field was one single sound. Not organized. Not rehearsed. Just the spontaneous expression of forty organizations who had been waiting all year for a day when being Filipino wasn't a background detail but the entire point. You could feel the pride through the phone. It was overwhelming in the best way, the kind of overwhelming that doesn't feel like too much, it feels like exactly enough. That moment opened the door for me to advance at the station earlier than I expected. But what I carried out of Friendship Games wasn't a career win. It was something harder to name and longer lasting. The proof that when you show up for the right room, the room shows up for you.

Labor Before Legacy

There is a specific kind of contribution that happens in Filipino cultural spaces that most brands never see because they arrive after the work is already done. They show up for the event, the launch, the moment, and they miss everything that made the moment possible.

What they miss is the labor. The hours of unpaid preparation, the volunteers who arrived early and stayed late, the designers who created the visual identity for free, the DJs who drove hours to play a thirty-minute set because the community needed the music, the organizers who handled logistics on personal phones with no budget and no staff. This is the invisible infrastructure of Filipino cultural events, and it runs entirely on a logic that has nothing to do with compensation or recognition. It runs on the understanding that the community builds what it needs because nobody else is going to build it.

I am one of those DJs. Not in theory. In practice, across years of showing up before anyone offered to pay me for it.

At Wild 107 / 94.9 in San Francisco, I was in the rooms before Filipino culture was a brand category. I volunteered to DJ our community remote activations. I got involved with Filipino clubs at colleges across the Bay Area, meeting their teams, their boards, getting to know the people doing the work. I DJed community events for free. Filipino festivals. Philippine Culture Nights. PCNs that ran on student labor and collective pride and absolutely no budget. I did it not because I was building a brand or chasing exposure but because it felt right. And underneath that feeling was something I didn't fully have language for at the time: I had grown up without many role models who looked like me in the spaces I wanted to occupy. By being present, by MC-ing and DJing and showing up in rooms where Filipino students could see someone who had made it through, I was trying to be the thing I hadn't had. Someone they could see themselves in.

We were one of the most powerful Top Rhythmic stations in the Bay Area and I used every ounce of that platform to make sure Filipino artists and Filipino spaces felt the weight of it. Friendship Games. GoodPhil. Community events that our competitors didn't know existed or didn't think were worth the trip. I thought they were worth the trip every single time.

At Z90 in San Diego, I brought the same frequency to a different market and did the same thing. San Diego has one of the largest Filipino populations in the country and a community that had been building something real for decades without much mainstream radio acknowledgment. I showed up to Filipino community events, festivals, college nights, the same way I had in the Bay. Because I worked for the station, I used my platform to be there for the culture. Being in those rooms, with that platform behind me, mattered in ways that didn't show up in any ratings report.

And then there was Wild 106 in San Luis Obispo. My friend DJ Mel and I were both from the Bay. We were both Filipino. And we both saw the same gap when we looked at what the weekend mixshow could be and what it actually was. So we teamed up and leveled it up. Two Bay Area kids in a college market, doing what we knew how to do, because we had the platform and it felt wrong not to use it. Some people call that paying dues. We just called it Tuesday.

I also spoke at college Filipino clubs and high school conferences for years, because the students needed someone who had been in those rooms before them and made it through. And I worked on the branding and design of community events because I could see the gap between what these events looked like and what they deserved to look like. I wanted to help move them from being perceived as low budget to being seen as the world-class cultural productions they actually were. Not because anyone asked me to. Because the community had given me something I could not put a dollar value on, and this was the only way I knew how to give it back.

Some people have told me I was being used. I have experienced versions of that too. But the way I understand it, and the way I have watched other Filipino DJs and creators understand it, is closer to *Utang na loob*, the Filipino concept of a debt of gratitude, the understanding that what the community gave you cannot be repaid to the individual who gave it. It can only be paid forward to the next person who needs it. The community built the floor you're standing on. The labor is how you prove you know that.

The brands that understand this, that see the labor and honor it before they ask for anything, are the ones that actually get invited in. Not because they paid for the right, but because they demonstrated that they understood what it cost to build the thing they wanted to be part of.

That understanding is what separates a genuine participant from a well-resourced tourist.

The Non-Filipino Twenty Percent

One of the most consistent signals that a Filipino cultural event has achieved genuine belonging rather than just community service is what happens at the edges of the crowd.

At GoodPhil, roughly twenty percent of the attendees were not Filipino. They didn't come because a brand reached them with a targeted ad or because an algorithm served them the event. They came because someone in their life, a Filipino friend, a coworker, a partner, brought them. They were guests in the truest sense: invited by residents who felt confident enough in the environment to share it with someone from outside it.

That twenty percent is the most important metric in the room, and it has nothing to do with diversity or inclusion as a brand objective. It's proof that the frequency is strong enough to travel, that what was built for the resident is resonant enough that the tourist wants to understand it. When non-Filipinos are in a

Filipino cultural space and they're not confused or performing their appreciation but genuinely present and genuinely moved, it means the culture isn't performing either. It's just being itself. And being itself is the highest possible standard.

A brand that helps create the conditions for that twenty percent to show up, not by diluting the culture to make it more accessible, but by making the resident feel so seen and so centered that they want to share the experience, has achieved something that no demographic targeting strategy can manufacture. It has helped build a room worth inviting people into.

BAHAY KUBO LOGIC

*What a bamboo house
teaches about belonging*

In the influence model, a brand is built like a skyscraper, a rigid, glass-and-steel monument designed to be seen from a distance. It is impressive in the way that things built to intimidate are impressive. It dominates the skyline through sheer scale, demanding recognition without inviting participation. You can look at it. You cannot touch it. You certainly cannot move it. It was never built to be carried.

In the belonging model, a brand must be built like a Bahay Kubo.

The Bahay Kubo is the indigenous stilt house of the Philippines, and it is far more sophisticated than it looks from the outside. It is an engineering solution to an environment defined by volatility, monsoons, floods, shifting earth, the kind of conditions that would crack a concrete foundation in a season. It is light, modular, and built with the understanding that permanence isn't about rigidity. It's about the ability to move with the world rather than against it. And when a family needs to relocate, the neighborhood doesn't just watch from a respectful distance. They show up, they lift the house onto their shoulders, and they carry it together. That is Bayanihan, the physical, communal act of belonging made visible.

To build a brand that a community is willing

to carry, you have to understand the three structural pillars that make the Kubo work.

The first pillar is the *Haligi*, the stilts. These are the heavy timber posts that lift the house above the mud and the floodwaters, the elements that keep the whole structure from sinking under pressure. In branding, the *Haligi* are your core values, the only parts of the house that are genuinely non-negotiable. Most brands have this completely backwards. They stay fluid about their values to chase trends while remaining rigid about their aesthetic, protecting the logo and the color palette with the ferocity they should be reserving for their purpose. *Kubo Logic* reverses this entirely. The aesthetic can breathe. The values cannot move. You must be immovable in your purpose so that you are elevated enough to see the landscape clearly and grounded enough to withstand the pressure of a community audit that will test everything you claim to stand for. If your *Haligi* are weak or performative, if the values are marketing language rather than operational reality, the community will never risk standing under your roof. They've seen too many roofs collapse.

The second pillar is the *Silong*, the open space underneath the house. In traditional Filipino architecture, the *Silong* is used for storage, for livestock, for communal work, a shared space that the structure provides but doesn't police. Nobody owns the *Silong* exclusively. It belongs to whoever needs it. In branding, the *Silong* is the part of your platform that you don't monetize, don't over-brand, and don't subtitle. It is the unclaimed space you leave for the community to use on their own terms, for their own purposes, without a corporate watermark attached. If you're a music label, it's the stems you release for free remixing. If you're a retail brand, it's the empty gallery wall you let the local kids paint without approval processes and brand guidelines. The *Silong* is your proof that you are not there to extract every possible unit of value from the relationship. If you don't provide one, you aren't a resident. You're a closed door with a logo on it.

The final pillar is the *Dingding*, the walls. In the Bahay Kubo, the walls are made of light nipa or bamboo, designed to be moved, repaired, or replaced entirely as the environment requires. They allow the house to breathe. They are functional, beautiful, and impermanent by design, because the people who built this house understood that flexibility isn't weakness. It's survival. This is where most corporate entities fail completely. They treat their brand guidelines like poured concrete, immovable and identical in every market, every community, every context. Kubo Logic says the opposite: your visual identity must be permissive. You must allow the community to repaint your brand, remix your assets, adapt your aesthetic to fit the specific neighborhood they actually live in. When you allow the community to change the exterior of your brand, they stop seeing it as a corporate billboard that was installed without their consent and start seeing it as something they had a hand in building. Something that, in some real sense, belongs to them.

When cultural collaborations fail, it is almost always because the brand brought *Concrete Logic* into a Kubo environment.

The Global Flag error is the most common version of this. A sports organization wants to celebrate a Heritage Night, a genuine desire, real intent, real budget. But instead of applying Kubo Logic, inviting local designers to create something modular, something that reflects the specific soul of that neighborhood and that community, they do what their brand guidelines allow them to do. They take the existing corporate colors and put a flag in the logo. The walls stayed concrete. The *Silong* was never offered. The *Haligi*, the actual values, the real commitment to the community, were never tested because the whole thing was designed to minimize exposure rather than maximize connection. And the community was expected to carry a structure that was never designed with them in mind, that was never light enough to lift, that had no place for their hands to grip.

They didn't carry it. Nobody was surprised.

To build for the next generation, you have to stop building monuments and start building homes. A house light enough to be carried. Stilts strong enough to stand the truth. Walls thin enough to let the community's own breath pass through.

*If you don't provide a Silong,
you aren't a resident. You're a
closed door with a logo on it.*

You belong, or you don't. And the community has always known which one you are before you've finished your pitch.

HOW BELONGING IS BUILT

Recognition is the spark. Participation is the invitation. But in my experience, the spark is the easy part. Any brand with a good creative team and the right cultural consultant can produce a moment that lands, a campaign that feels true, an activation that generates real energy, a Heritage Night that the community actually shows up for. What comes after the spark is where almost everyone loses the thread.

The real challenge is the burn.

Belonging isn't a viral moment or a high-production giveaway or even a genuinely well-executed event. It's a cumulative state, the result of building something that keeps standing long after the media spend has dried up and the campaign flight has ended and the internal team has moved on to the next quarter's objectives. It's infrastructure, not activation. And if you want to move from a temporary interaction to something that actually lives inside a community, you have to stop thinking in campaigns and start thinking in environments.

We're going deep into Contribution first, the process by which a brand stops extracting value from a cultural environment and starts genuinely producing it. Then we look at Signals, the details that tell a community whether you actually understand the world you're trying to enter. And finally Continuity, the factor that transforms a single well-intentioned moment into something durable enough to outlast any individual campaign.

But before any of that, there's a choice every brand has to make. It's not a strategic choice or a creative one. It's an identity choice.

You are either the Host or the Tool.

When a brand operates as the Host, it provides the

infrastructure the neighborhood needs, the space, the production value, the resources that make the environment better than it would be without them. It stops being a product trying to reach an audience and starts being the scene itself. They don't need to put their logo everywhere because their presence is already felt in the quality of the environment they helped create.

When a brand operates as the Tool, it gets out of its own way entirely. It stops talking about itself and starts providing the language, the platform, the canvas through which the community expresses its own identity. It's the brush, not the painting. And the community picks it up because it works, not because it was marketed to them.

One brand says: come into my world. The other says: build your world through mine. Both are valid. Both can create genuine residency. What neither can afford to do is show up as something in between, present enough to take up space, but not committed enough to actually contribute to the floor.

Every community is running a constant, silent energy audit on every brand that enters its space. They are evaluating not just what you brought but what you took, not just whether you showed up but why, not just what the collaboration looked like from the outside but what it felt like from the inside. If the audit determines you were there to extract attention, you get flagged as an intruder. If it determines you were there to contribute something real, you start the slow, necessary process of becoming a resident.

That audit never stops running. Which means the work never stops either.

Here's how it actually gets built.

Influence is a tool.
Belonging is an environment.

CHAPTER 7

Contribution: Add, Don't Extract

—

Participation gets you through the door. It does not determine what happens once you're inside.

Those are not the same thing, and the community knows the difference faster than any brand is usually prepared for.

This is where Contribution becomes the deciding factor. It defines the quality of the involvement, the weight of what's being put in: time, attention, creativity, resources, genuine understanding. If participation is about having a role, contribution is about what you actually do with it. And in cultural environments, where identity is the stakes, that distinction is everything.

The Energy Audit

Every community is running a constant, silent energy audit on every brand that enters its space. Not just at the beginning, not just during the launch moment, but continuously. Every interaction, every decision, every signal the brand sends about why it's actually there gets logged and evaluated. Most brands focus on participation metrics without ever honestly addressing the weight of what they're contributing. They create opportunities for engagement that don't improve the environment in any meaningful way. They generate activity that looks good on a quarterly report and leaves the community exactly where it found them. Empty calories dressed up as nourishment.

The Audit in Real-Time: Forgotten Island

The most instructive recent example of this audit running in public is the community's response to DreamWorks' *Forgotten Island*, a film that matters not just because of what it is, but because of how it came to exist.

Forgotten Island is directed by Joel Crawford and Januel Mercado, the same filmmaking team behind the Oscar-nominated *Puss in Boots: The Last Wish*. Mercado is Filipino-American, raised in Northern California, who grew up knowing the scary parts of Filipino folklore, the stories parents use to keep children in line, but not the full depth of the mythology. Crawford is what the community would call an honorary Filipino: his wife grew up in the Philippines until she was nine, and it was her stories about the *manananggal* and the *tikbalang* and the creatures of Filipino mythology that first made him realize there was something here worth building a film around.

They didn't get handed this project. They pitched it, an original, personal story rooted in Filipino folklore, built in the same visual style they'd already proven they could execute at the highest level. And when they took it to DreamWorks, they got the same question that Jo Koy got from Netflix, that every Filipino creator eventually gets from the gatekeepers: where's the explosions? Where are the car chases? How is a culturally specific story about friendship and memory supposed to be a big Hollywood movie?

Their answer is the same one Jo Koy gave when he bet his life savings on *Live from Seattle*: the specificity is the point, not the problem. Crawford described their goal simply. They want people to walk out of the theater and call their best friend. Not their Filipino best friend. Just their best friend. The Filipino mythology isn't a barrier to universality. It's the specific, original, never-before-seen vehicle for getting there. Once you get past the initial unfamiliarity, once you realize that the *manananggal* is a vampire and the *tikbalang* is a horseman and the Philippines has its own versions of every archetype Western audiences already love, the commonality becomes obvious. And the specificity is what makes it feel like something genuinely new rather than another sequel to something you've already seen.

That origin matters enormously to how the community runs its audit. This wasn't a studio deciding Filipino culture was trending and commissioning something to capitalize on the moment. It was filmmakers using the credibility they'd earned at the top of their industry to get a story made that they actually cared about, one that came from real proximity, real personal connection, real time spent inside the culture before anyone started writing the script.

Then there's the cast: H.E.R., Liza Soberano, Lea Salonga, Dolly de Leon, Jo Koy, and Manny Jacinto. On the surface, a tourist looks at that lineup and sees Filipino representation, the visual markers, the mythology, the *balisong* and the jeepney in the trailer, and calls it a win. And in one sense it is. But the community's audit goes immediately and instinctively deeper than the surface.

What the community saw in that cast was a studio making a structural decision to put Filipino talent at the center of a global platform, not as window dressing but as the actual architecture of the film. That's the brand acting as a genuine Host, giving their people not just a moment of visibility but real creative real estate in a major production. The combination of filmmakers who fought to get this made and a cast of that caliber signals something the community doesn't hear from studios very often: we took this seriously enough to do it right. That gets the community to the table.

But the audit doesn't stop there. It never does. Almost immediately, the conversation shifted to a deeper interrogation: Is this based on *Biringan*? Is that accurate? Does the mythology hold up to what we actually know? From the outside, that can look like nitpicking. From the inside, it's the community doing exactly what it's supposed to do, determining whether this offering actually belongs to them, whether it was built with enough understanding of the world it's drawing from to deserve to be called Filipino rather than just Filipino-adjacent. Scheduled for release on September 25, 2026, the film hasn't had its final verdict yet. But the early signal is clear: the community is paying attention at a depth that most studios never anticipate, because most studios never earn it.

The cast gets them to the table. The narrative depth, the accuracy of the folklore, the integrity of the mythology, the degree to which the story actually mirrors the lived experience of the diaspora, determines whether they stay.

The Immigrant Narrative as Value

What brands consistently miss when they think about contribution is that the most valuable thing they can offer isn't always the production budget or the platform or the talent lineup. Sometimes the most powerful contribution is the recognition of a lived experience that the community has been carrying quietly for a long time without seeing reflected back at them at scale.

In *Forgotten Island*, the story of characters being pulled into another world, navigating the space between where they came from and where they are now, the desperate effort not to lose who they are in the process of becoming something new, mirrors the Filipino immigrant experience with a precision that doesn't need to be explained to anyone who has lived it. Growing up between two worlds. Growing apart from one while trying to hold onto both. That internal reality, rendered in a story, stops being content and becomes something closer to a gift. It says: we saw this, we understood it, and we thought it was worth telling.

That's the distinction between extraction and gifting. Extraction takes from the cultural library, the aesthetics, the cool, the visibility boost, without putting anything back. Gifting adds to it. It gives the community a tool, a narrative, a mirror that helps them see themselves more clearly or more fully than they could before.

The Compounding Effect: The Golden State Model

The clearest example I've seen of contribution done right, sustained, structural, genuinely compounding over time, is the Golden State Warriors' relationship with the Filipino community.

For most professional sports franchises, a Heritage Night is a checklist item. A branded t-shirt, a flag in the logo, a social media post in the week leading up to the game. That's extraction: the franchise takes the community's cultural identity and uses it to sell tickets for one night, and then the relationship ends until next year's Heritage Night needs a theme. The community shows up because they love the team, not because the team has done anything to earn a deeper connection. The transaction is completed, the box is checked, and everyone moves on.

The Warriors did something different. They treated the Filipino community not as an annual activation opportunity but as a permanent residency, a constituency that deserved a year-round relationship, not a Heritage Night. They built a system: long-term creative collaborations with cultural residents like P-Lo, sustained presence at community events like Pistahan, a consistency of engagement that communicated something the community doesn't hear from brands very often. We're here because we want to be here, not because the calendar told us to be.

When P-Lo stands at center court during a Warriors game, what's happening is not an advertisement for a rapper or a basketball team. It's a meaning-transfer platform, proof that the community's culture and the franchise's identity have genuinely merged, because the Warriors did the work of contribution before they ever asked for the community's attention. And because of that, the community now carries the Warriors as a badge of their own identity. The brand doesn't have to push anymore. The community pulls.

That's what contribution compounds into when you sustain it long enough. Not just goodwill, but genuine belonging, the kind that gets carried forward by the community itself, long after any individual campaign has ended.

The Right Version: The Yankees Jacket

The contrast to every Heritage Night giveaway that misses is the 2025 New York Yankees Filipino Heritage bomber jacket, and what makes it worth studying isn't just the design. It's the decision that preceded it.

The Yankees are one of the most conservative franchises in professional sports. They have resisted mascots, city connect jerseys, and virtually every design departure from their century-old aesthetic. When they decided to do a Filipino Heritage Night, they made a choice that most teams with far less institutional rigidity haven't made: they handed the creative entirely to a Filipino designer and told him to make the best Filipino Heritage giveaway he could.

That designer was Mark Anthony Agbuya, a second-generation Fil-Am who has been behind Filipino Heritage Night merchandise for East Coast franchises including the Yankees, Brooklyn Nets, and New York Knicks. What he created was not a flag stuffed into a logo. On the outside, the jacket is navy blue with the Yankees NY emblem embedded directly inside the Philippine sun on the chest, two identities fused into a single symbol, neither one subordinate to the other. The Philippine flag appears as a small patch on the sleeve, present but understated. Turn the jacket inside out and the entire lining becomes the Philippine flag, full blue, red, and white with the sun and stars across the whole back. The signal is there for the resident at every layer. The tourist sees a Yankees jacket. The resident sees the whole story.

Mark told me something that stayed with me. He does all of this for free. He gives it back to the community, here in the States or in the Philippines. He calls it paying it forward. Positive Pinoy. He described himself simply as a real Filipino who cares about the next generation.

The event sold out. People wanted the jacket. I wanted one.

That same weekend, I connected Mark and the New York Filipino community to Hillari, a Filipino artist who was making her debut concert in New York at the same time. Not because there was a deal to make or a campaign to run, because that's how this ecosystem actually works. The Heritage Night, the concert, the jacket, the community connections, none of it was manufactured from a brief. It all moved through the same network, carried by people who show up because the culture is worth showing up for.

That's the difference between a Heritage Night that sells out and one that doesn't. It's not the budget. It's whether the brand trusted the community enough to hand over the creative, and whether the person who received that trust was building for the community rather than for themselves.

The Introduction of this book opens with a hat that didn't sell because the soul was stripped out of it. The Yankees jacket is what happens when the soul is put back in.

Shaping the Environment

The shift that contribution produces, when it's real and sustained, is a fundamental change in the brand's relationship to the environment. It stops being an external entity seeking attention and becomes part of the system that produces value for the community. Its presence is defined not by what it's trying to get but by what it consistently adds.

But here's the thing about contribution that even well-intentioned brands get wrong: you can invest heavily in the what, the project, the production, the partnership, the platform, and still fail the audit entirely if you get the how wrong. You can bring the most thoughtful, expensive gift to the housewarming and still signal that you don't understand the house you're in, just by showing up in a tuxedo to a backyard BBQ. The gift doesn't save you from the signal. The community doesn't separate what you brought from how you brought it. They experience both simultaneously, and the how carries at least as much weight as the what.

Contribution provides the fuel. But the next pillar, Signals, is what determines whether the community recognizes that fuel as theirs. Without the right shorthand, the right codes, the right proof that you understand the world you're operating in at a granular level, even the most genuine contribution can feel like a loud, expensive mistake.

CHAPTER 8

Signals: The Handshake

—

Contribution determines what gets added to an environment. Signals determine whether the community recognizes it as theirs.

They are the granular codes, the subtle, layered identifiers that operate beneath the surface of every cultural interaction. In a corporate brief, this gets called Brand Identity. On the ground, it's the vibe check, the way a room sounds when the cameras are off, the specific way a varsity jacket sits on a shoulder, the shorthand reference that lands without needing a punchline because everyone in the room already lives inside the same world. Signals establish what belongs and what doesn't. They define what's normal and what's an intrusion. And the friction almost always starts at the same place: when a brand tries to buy its way into the room rather than becoming the room. That's where the signals cross, and when signals cross in a high-context cultural environment, the failure of tone is immediate and often irreversible.

The Cool Parent Paradox

Because signals are tied to behavior rather than aesthetics, they are notoriously difficult to replicate from a spreadsheet or a trend report. You can study the output of a culture, the music, the fashion, the language, the visual codes, and still produce something that feels completely wrong to everyone inside it, because what you're capturing is the surface and what the community is evaluating is the soul.

This is the root of Cultural Tourism, and it follows a predictable pattern. A legacy brand realizes its core audience is aging out. The urgency kicks in. They pivot toward a younger demographic with the same broadcast mindset they've always used, treating the next generation as a commodity to be reached rather than a culture to be joined. And the first question they ask when they approach a creator isn't how can we add value to what you're building. It's how can you help us reach your audience. That question, delivered in that order, is the ultimate intruder signal.

Zero-Captioning: The Sovereign Handshake

The most powerful signals are the ones you refuse to translate.

There's a specific kind of cultural confidence that comes with leaving something untranslated, the decision to have a private conversation in public, to speak directly to the people who understand and let everyone else catch up or not. It's the signal that says: this moment is for the residents, and we trust the residents to find it without a caption.

The two-week arc of BINI at Coachella 2026 is the most complete demonstration of this principle I've seen play out in real time at a global scale. Week One was what I'd call the Infiltration, BINI establishing Recognition in a space that didn't yet know their name. English introductions, high-gloss pop spectacle, the professional competence of artists who know how to read a room and meet it where it is. They were guests testing the frequency, proving they could operate in the space before they changed the terms of it.

Week Two was something else entirely. The crowd was bigger. More Blooms. More Philippine flags visible before the set even started. You could feel the shift in the room before they played a single note. And from the first moment, they made it clear they weren't going to ease into anything. The room was going to meet them instead.

Having proven they could play the game, they stopped playing it. They stripped the corporate translation layer completely and moved into what I can only describe as total Cultural Sovereignty. Instead of English introductions, each member spoke in her own native dialect. Maloi opened with a Batangueño "*Ala-eh!*" Gwen shouted a Bicolano "*Oragon!*" Aiah and Colet commanded the Coachella desert in Bisaya: "*Shagit og kusog!*" Stacey greeted the crowd in Ilocano: "*Naimbag nga aldaw, ading!*" They weren't just speaking their languages. They were sending a beacon across ten thousand miles to every Filipino in that crowd and every Filipino watching the stream, a signal that said: we didn't come here to be translated. We came here to be recognized.

And then came the moment that made everything else make sense. When they said "We are BINI, all the way from..." they didn't even finish the line. The entire tent shouted it back: "the Philippines." Not just the Filipino fans. The whole room. That doesn't come from hype or production or the right lighting cue. That comes from something that was already connecting before anyone said a word, a community that had been building toward this moment and a crowd that had felt enough of the frequency to know exactly what came next.

Their confidence after that was different. They carried themselves like people who knew the room would respond, and because of that, they pushed it further, got the entire tent jumping, making noise, moving together. It stopped feeling like a performance you were watching and started feeling like something you were part of. That's not a production outcome. That's belonging, happening in real time, at scale, in the middle of a desert.

By refusing to translate, they forced the global audience to catch their frequency rather than the other way around. They achieved something that most brands spend millions trying to manufacture and never get close to: Institutional Validation not by fitting into Coachella, but by making Coachella fit into them. When they took their final bow with the Philippine flag filling the jumbo screen and closed with *"Mabuhay ang musikang Pilipino,"* nothing needed to be explained. They proved something the industry is still struggling to fully absorb: the more specific you are to your home, the more the world wants to live there.

And the part most brands miss entirely: they didn't step back from who they were to reach more people. They went deeper into it. More language. More identity. More of where they actually came from. And instead of losing the room, they pulled more of it in. We tend to assume growth requires simplifying, translating, making things more accessible to a broader audience. What BINI demonstrated is that what actually scales is something people can genuinely feel part of. They didn't change for the room. The room met them where they were.

Sovereign Aesthetics and the Eyyy

True residency is defined by what I call *Sovereign Aesthetics*, the refusal to use heritage as a theatrical prop, the insistence on deploying cultural codes on your own terms rather than translating them for maximum accessibility.

When BINI projected the eight-rayed sun and three stars on the Coachella screens, they made a deliberate choice: they stripped away the blue and red of the Philippine national flag and presented the symbols alone, in gold, against the desert sky. To a tourist, it was just a graphic, a nod to Filipino heritage, visually striking, easy to photograph. To a resident, it was a high-context signal of a completely different order. It was the visual equivalent of the dialect introductions: a declaration that the culture is sovereign, that it doesn't require a full translation to be valid, that the community doesn't need permission from the mainstream to exist at full resolution.

This same logic extends to what became known as the *Eyyy*, the phrase and hand gesture popularized by BINI's Sheena Catacutan that spread through the Coachella campgrounds and across social media and eventually became inseparable from the group's identity. The gesture itself is the *shaka*, Hawaii's universal symbol of aloha, a sign of warmth and ease that has traveled across cultures. But the *Eyyy* isn't the *shaka*. BINI took a universal gesture and gave it a specifically Filipino soul, and the moment it was born tells you everything about how signals actually work.

It didn't start on a stage. It started at a fan meet, when a fan told Sheena she was about to graduate college and was already emotional about it. Sheena's response was immediate and completely instinctive: "*Naiiyak ka? Eyyy ka muna, eyyy!*" Essentially: you're crying? Hold on, do the *Eyyy* first. Celebrate before you cry. The phrase spread because it captured something specific about how Filipinos move through emotion, the communal insistence on joy, the refusal to let someone feel alone in a difficult moment, the warmth that shows up before it's asked for. By the time BINI performed at Coachella, the *Eyyy* had already been living inside the community for months. When it spread through the campgrounds and across social media during the festival weekend, it wasn't manufactured. It was already theirs. As of April 2026, searching BINI on Google triggers eight *Eyyy* emojis. The algorithm had absorbed the signal as inseparable from the group itself. That's not a marketing outcome. That's a cultural frequency recognized at the institutional level.

A broadcast is a song. A participatory signal is a gesture that spreads on its own because the community has claimed it, and this one started with one artist telling one fan: *eyyy ka muna.*

Hacking the Heritage

In high-context culture, some of the most powerful signals are the ones you wear on your body, and specifically, the ones you wear on your feet.

When a brand operates as a genuine Host, it stops trying to design for a community and starts allowing residents to embed codes that only another resident can fully decrypt. DJ Javier did this with Vans. He took the checkerboard, one of the most sacred symbols in skate culture, and redesigned it into the *Checkerbayan*, embedding the sun and stars directly into the rubber sole and placing the Carabao on the heel. He anchored Southern California counter-culture to the grit of the Philippine rice fields in a single design, creating something that reads as skate culture to the outsider and as something much more specific and much more personal to the resident.

The same resident logic extended to DJ Javier's work with LAFC and the LA Kings, and what makes those collaborations worth examining specifically is the depth of the trust the franchises extended. He didn't just design the promotional giveaway item for Heritage Night. He designed the exclusive merchandise sold in the stadium stores. That distinction matters enormously. A giveaway is a Heritage Night gesture, present for one night, gone by morning. Merchandise in the permanent store is an institutional statement: this belongs here year-round, not just when the calendar says Filipino Heritage Night. By giving DJ Javier both, the franchises were saying something the community heard immediately, that his creative vision wasn't a seasonal decoration but a permanent part of how they represent themselves to their fans.

Louis De Guzman's *Ma Divina* collaboration with New Balance operates on the same frequency but through a completely different visual language. The soft lavenders and sky blues of that shoe are geometric abstractions of the floral arrangements his mother made to survive in Chicago, a story of immigrant resilience rendered in color and silhouette. To the outsider, it's a beautiful sneaker. To the resident, it's the immigrant in-between, worn on the street, carried forward. And Rich Tu's *First Generation* project at Nike took this signaling to an institutional level, using the graphic shorthand of the Hand and the Eye to speak directly to everyone who has ever felt like the first in their room, the first in their family, the first of their name in a space that wasn't built with them in mind.

None of these brands hired influencers to post photos of the product. They allowed cultural residents to hack their heritage into the brand's most valuable assets, and in doing so, they created signals that the community carries forward because the community helped build them.

The Signal in the Room: Hillari

There is a version of this that doesn't happen on a Coachella stage or in a global sneaker collaboration. It happens in a conference hall in Ottawa, Canada, in front of a room that has never heard your name.

Hillari is a Filipino-Norwegian R&B and soul artist, Bagonhon by birth, raised in *Barangay* Poblacion in Bago City in the Visayas, whose mother's love of music shaped her sound from the beginning. She is what researchers call an Adult Third Culture Kid, someone formed by multiple worlds simultaneously, who belongs fully to none of them and draws from all of them. She spent her early childhood in the Philippines from ages three to eight, entertained relatives and neighbors who gathered at her family's house, and built her first relationship with performance not on a stage but in a living room. She carried that foundation to Norway as a teenager, started her music career at eighteen, released her debut EP *How is Your Soul*, performed at Norway's largest festival, and won the country's NRK P3 Artist of the Year, all in the same year. In March 2025, she won the *Spellemannprisen*, the Norwegian Grammy, Norway's most prestigious music award established in 1973, for R&B/Soul. She was nineteen.

Her sound carries both worlds without explaining either. She's described it simply: "Without my Norwegian and Filipina background, I don't think I would have had the same originality in my sound, or would carry myself in the same way." In Norway she navigated *Janteloven*, the societal norm that says don't think you're too original, don't get too caught up thinking you're better than anyone else, because everybody is the same. She brought that quietly confident mindset into LA rooms that reward the opposite. "When I'm in rooms in LA, sometimes I'm encouraged to own what I'm doing more," she says. "But I like having this mindset because it keeps me quietly confident."

That tension, between Norwegian restraint and Filipino communal warmth, is exactly what makes her signal so specific. When asked what her favorite thing about being Filipino is, her answer didn't go to food or music or any of the usual surface markers. She said: "the community." Specifically: "I love how Filipinos show up for each other, especially in this age of just hyper-independence. We're so family oriented in the Philippines, while in Norway we're very hyper-independent. The more I grew up, the more I see my dependence on having people I love around me." That's not a marketing quote. That's someone who has lived inside both cultures and can feel the gap between them, and who has chosen, consciously, which frequency to run on.

During a visit to the Bago City mayor's office, she said it in Hiligaynon, without prompting: "I will always be a proud Bagonhon, a part that I will never let go. *Taga diri gid ko ya*, this is where I was formed much, this is where my values were formed." That's not a brand moment. That's a frequency, and it's the same one the community recognizes before she sings a single note.

I watched this happen firsthand at Pinoys on Parliament in Ottawa in 2025. She performed for a room that didn't know her name going in. She left with over 350 new fans. Not followers. Fans, people who felt something real and chose to carry it forward. That's not a visibility outcome. That's a signal landing.

The signal doesn't need to be loud. It needs to be accurate. And when it's accurate, the room recognizes it before it can explain why.

Later, when Hillari prepared for her debut concert in New York, her team had limited contacts on the ground in the Filipino community. I connected her to the network, to Venessa at the

Filipino School of New York and New Jersey, to Jason and Kat of Future Ancestors, to Mark Anthony Agbuya, who was running the Yankees Filipino Heritage Night that same weekend. Mark took care of her. He made sure she had a jacket. The Filipino community showed up for her concert the way the Filipino community shows up for its own, not because a campaign told them to, but because the frequency had already been established and the network carried the signal forward.

That's how signals work at the community level. They don't require infrastructure. They require accuracy. When the frequency is right, the community does the distribution.

Programming vs. Presence

There's a specific failure mode that even well-resourced, genuinely well-intentioned brands fall into, and it's worth naming directly: the mistake of trying to program an organic moment.

It looks like this. A brand wants to show up authentically in a cultural space, so they hire the right talent, bring in a production crew, build out a content schedule, and execute everything at a high technical level. The result is something that is perfectly produced and completely out of place, a show dropped into the middle of a happening, a broadcast signal fired into a participatory environment. The talent delivers. The content gets made. And the moment the talent is off the clock, the audience evaporates, because the brand itself never established a resonant frequency. The talent was borrowed. The spotlight was rented. And when the rental period ends, there's nothing left to hold the brand in place because it never actually became part of the environment. It just performed inside it for a designated window of time.

That's not presence. That's tourism with a production budget.

You cannot build a residency on a campaign flight or a Heritage Month. You can build a moment. Moments are worth something. But moments aren't belonging. To turn a moment into something that lasts, you have to solve for what comes after the signal. You have to solve for presence that continues when there's no launch to justify it, no quarter to hit, no Heritage Night on the calendar.

You have to solve for Continuity.

CHAPTER 9

Continuity: Time Is The Deciding Factor

—

Recognition, Participation, Contribution, and Signals determine how something enters a cultural environment. Continuity determines whether it stays.

Without it, everything that came before is just a glitch, a temporary fit that felt real in the moment and evaporates the moment the activity stops. In the influence model, consistency is a chore, something performed to stay relevant in an algorithm, a cadence maintained because the platform punishes absence. In the residency model, Continuity is something different entirely. It's the act of becoming a reliable point in a cultural constellation, something the community can orient around, something that's still there when they look up, not because a campaign is running but because that's simply where you live.

The Bituin Shift: From Spotlight to Constellation

The highest metric of Continuity isn't reach or impressions or even engagement. It's the transition from Attendance to Return, the shift from showing up once to being someone the community expects to see again.

I understand this shift through the Tagalog word *Bituin*, star. I was in Ottawa, Canada for Pinoys on Parliament, a Filipino leadership conference, there to DJ and speak. The theme of the conference was *Bituin*, and before I went on stage, I had to ask someone what it meant.

That detail matters. Four years of returning to this event, and I was still learning something new from it.

When I found out it meant star, my first instinct was the obvious one, achievement, visibility, standing out. The broadcast model's definition of success applied to a Tagalog word. But as the weekend unfolded, that meaning started to shift, and by the time I walked into the gala that evening, wearing a *barong* alongside dozens of others, hearing the natural back-and-forth of Tagalog and English in every conversation around me, smelling food that had become familiar over four years of returning to this same room, the word stopped being a question about visibility and became something else entirely.

It became a realization about where I already was.

A star on its own is just light. But stars together become something you can navigate by. *Bituin* wasn't about standing out. It was about realizing you're part of a constellation.

That shift didn't happen in a single moment. It happened the way continuity always works, gradually, through accumulation, through the specific weight of the fourth year feeling different from the first because the people in the room had become a family of friends rather than a gathering of strangers. At dinner that night, there were seven of us at the table, some meeting for the first time, some acquaintances who had crossed paths at previous events. By the end of the meal, none of those categories applied anymore. We were sharing real stories, real pivots, real doubts, wins that hadn't been announced publicly yet. That dinner table became a network not because anyone intended it to but because four years of consistent presence had built the conditions for that kind of trust to form quickly.

Continuity turns a room full of strangers into a family of friends. It is the shift from fighting to be seen to simply finding the rooms where you already exist, where your presence is expected rather than performed.

The Pulse of the Room

Most marketing is built on the Burst, a tightly defined window of high-intensity activity followed by silence, engineered around a launch date or a campaign flight or a fiscal quarter. The burst is loud and visible and legible to internal stakeholders because it produces numbers within a defined timeframe. And then it ends, and the brand disappears, and the community moves on because that was always the implicit agreement.

Culture doesn't move on a burst. Culture moves on a Pulse.

The Pulse is the energy that exists in the gaps, what happens in the room when the programming breaks down, when the schedule falls apart, when nobody is performing for the cameras anymore. The next day, at the showcase and after-party, I saw it firsthand. There was a production delay between sets, the kind of logistical breakdown that can kill the energy of a room in minutes if nothing fills the space. The crowd was calling for *Bebot* by Apl of the Black Eyed Peas. It had just gone viral again on TikTok, and they wanted it. I played it. And then I followed it up with something different.

I dropped *Mundo* by IV of Spades.

The entire room transformed into a choir. Every word, sung at full volume, by everyone in that space simultaneously, not because anyone told them to, not because it was on the program, but because that song had been living inside the community across the US, Canada, the Philippines, and the diaspora for years. When it came on in a room full of Filipinos who had been gathering together for years, it found the frequency that was already there and the room just opened up around it.

That moment wasn't manufactured. No marketing budget produced it. It was the sound of a shared frequency maintained across years and thousands of miles, proof that true resonance isn't found in the planned performance but in the room's capacity to generate its own energy when the plan falls apart. Residents don't need a product launch to show up for each other. They don't need a program to know what comes next. They understand, in a way that tourists never quite do, that the off-season, the quiet space between the bursts, the unremarkable Tuesday that nobody is documenting, is where the actual residency is earned.

The Fight Song Nobody Commissioned

The same system that carried *Mundo* across the diaspora is what carried EZ Mil's *Panalo*.

When EZ Mil performed *Panalo* on the Wish Bus, he did something that the Corporate Excuse Framework had been insisting wasn't possible for decades: he rapped in Tagalog, Ilocano, and Bisaya, three distinct Filipino languages, with a delivery so confident and so precise that you didn't need to understand every word to feel every word. When I first saw it I thought: this kid is hella dope. Not as analysis. As a gut reaction. The performance hit before the brain could catch up, which is exactly what belonging does.

Panalo means win. And what EZ Mil did with that word, the way he moved through it in three languages, the way the performance carried the specific weight of someone who understood exactly what they were saying and why it mattered, felt like a fight song. The kind you walk out to. The kind that belongs to you before you've even decided it does.

The Wish Bus performance spread the way the *Mundo* drop spread: laterally, without coordination, through the community's own internal logic. No label push. No campaign. Just a Filipino kid on a stationary bus, performing in the languages of his people, and the diaspora recognizing the frequency before anyone declared it a moment.

It was never a discovery. The frequency was already there.

The World-Building Anchor: Baryo Hi-Fi

Continuity isn't just about how often you show up. It's about the consistency of the world you invite people into when you do.

This is the distinction that Baryo Hi-Fi has built its entire identity around. While most Filipino cultural festivals operate on what I'd call the shoestring heritage template, scattered vendor booths, temporary aesthetics, the visual language of something assembled quickly and economically to serve a single weekend, Baryo Hi-Fi, led by a collective of operators including Miles Canares, Jennifer Taylor, Stephanie Ramos, Kristofferson San Pablo, and Rion Barcena, refuses that template entirely.

They prioritize the architecture of the environment: cohesive high-design signage, integrated brand elements, a custom-animated low-rider Jeepney that functions as both a cultural anchor and a visual statement about the standard they're holding. Every element of the world they build is consistent every time a resident enters it, because consistency at that level communicates something that inconsistency never can, that this world is permanent, that the standards are real and not situational, that the people who built it care about what it feels like to be inside it every single time.

That consistency is what allows institutional partners like Nike to enter Baryo Hi-Fi as peers rather than tourists. When an environment is built to a genuinely high standard and that standard never wavers, major brands don't tower over it. They fit within it. The environment sets the terms. The brand meets them. And the community doesn't just attend the event. They move in, because the world is stable enough and well-built enough to actually live inside.

The Resident Mindset

What Continuity ultimately produces is trust, the specific, durable kind of trust that comes from the community being able to predict your presence, from knowing that when they look for you, you'll be there, not because there's a product to launch or a Heritage Month on the calendar but because that's simply how you operate.

Belonging happens when people recognize themselves in the room, not when they recognize your logo on the banner outside it. It happens when culture is treated as a lived experience rather than a theme, and when that treatment is consistent not just during the activations but in all the unremarkable time between them. That's why a dinner table turns into a network. That's why a DJ set turns into a choir. That's why a conference, attended consistently enough over enough years, stops being an event and starts being home.

True resonance is the sound of a frequency that never turns off. It is the thread that runs through Recognition, Participation, Contribution, and Signals and ties them into something durable, work that doesn't just fit the moment but defines the era, a presence that doesn't just show up in the room but becomes part of how the room knows itself. Continuity is what turns a guest into a resident. And residency is what turns a brand into something the community is willing to carry.

Ownership: When It Becomes Theirs

—

Continuity allows a brand to remain present within an environment. Ownership determines whether that presence is actually accepted and carried forward by the people in it.

This is where the fundamental dynamic of the relationship shifts in a way that most brands are structurally unprepared for. Up to this point, the brand has been the primary driver, responsible for entering the space, aligning with its values, showing up consistently, building the signals that tell the community it belongs. All of that is necessary work. But it is still, at its core, the brand doing something. Ownership changes that trajectory entirely. It's the moment the environment itself begins to incorporate the brand into its own internal structure, not because the brand asked it to, but because the community decided it was theirs.

The Brand Custodian's Paradox

Here is the part that makes ownership genuinely difficult for most organizations to achieve: to get there, a brand has to be willing to let go of the very thing it has spent years protecting.

Once people begin to integrate something into their own lives, they inevitably shape how it evolves, remixing it, recontextualizing it, carrying it into spaces and situations the brand never planned for, using it in ways that have nothing to do with the original marketing intent. From a brand management perspective, this looks like a loss of control. From a belonging perspective, it is the whole point.

Most brand custodians are hired specifically to prevent this from happening, to protect the logo, the voice, the guidelines from any external interference. But in the Belonging Engine, that instinct works against the very outcome the brand is trying to achieve. The more you protect the brand from the community, the more you distance the community from the brand. A fortress is safe, but it is also empty. A park is messy and unpredictable, but it is full of life.

The Proxy Resident: Claiming the Platform

One of the most powerful expressions of ownership happens when the community decides to claim a mainstream platform as their own, when they see a resident enter a space that wasn't built for them and collectively decide that the outcome of that entry belongs to everyone who shares that residency.

Ruby Ibarra's victory at the 2025 NPR Tiny Desk Contest is the clearest recent example of this mechanism. Out of over 7,500 submissions, Ruby won with *"Bakunawa,"* an atmospheric, multilingual hip-hop track performed in English, Tagalog, and Bisaya, rooted in Philippine mythology. The *Bakunawa* is the dragon-like creature from Filipino folklore believed to swallow the moon, and Ruby used that image as a metaphor to reclaim the narrative for immigrants and people of color. She wrote the song while pregnant with her first child, building it as a message to the next generation, and she recorded it as an intergenerational collaboration with Filipina-Canadian artist Haniely "Han Han" Pabelo, Filipina-American rock pioneer June Millington, and Ouida.

She didn't simplify the language for the judges. She didn't translate the experience to make it more accessible to a mainstream institution. A Bay Area rapper, director, and former research scientist in biotechnology, Ruby walked into one of the most prestigious platforms in American music and performed entirely on her own terms, and in doing so she turned NPR's Tiny Desk into a Filipino front porch. Not just for the duration of the performance, but in the cultural memory of every Filipino who watched it. When she followed that win with a sold-out ten-city national tour, it wasn't just a career milestone. It was a victory lap for a community that had claimed a piece of the American musical infrastructure as their own.

This same mechanism is what drives the Filipino diaspora's legendary mobilization around global voting platforms. When Sofronio Vasquez won The Voice in late 2024, or when Jessica Sanchez returned to the America's Got Talent stage in 2025 to finally take the crown while nine months pregnant, the community wasn't passively watching television. They were colonizing the airwaves, turning corporate entertainment properties into effectively Filipino shows for the duration of those seasons, because they recognized a shared residency on the screen and refused to let the network decide who belonged at the top. The community took ownership of the outcome because ownership, in their experience, is not granted. It is claimed.

The Assigned Ownership Trap

When ownership is forced from the top down, assigned by an institution rather than earned through genuine residency, the community's response is almost always immediate and unambiguous rejection.

The appointment of Vanessa Hudgens as a Global Tourism Ambassador is a clear example of this dynamic. Hudgens is a massive star, and her Filipino heritage is real. But the title was granted institutionally, from the top down, without a foundation of consistent contribution or sustained engagement with the community that would have given it meaning. Because the community didn't feel a history of residency from her prior to the appointment, they read the whole thing as a Tourist signal, a title handed to a name rather than earned by a presence.

The Shay Mitchell situation cuts even deeper because it reveals something the community tracks very carefully: not just what you claim on the way up, but what you discard once you've arrived. Mitchell spent years positioning herself as a Filipino representative, including through her involvement in projects like Trese, where she cited her mother's Filipino heritage as the reason she took the role. Then, during the May 2024 premiere of her Max show Thirst, she described her background plainly: "My dad's Irish, my mom's Spanish." Her mother, Precious Garcia, is from Pampanga, Philippines. To the community, that wasn't a minor genealogical clarification. It was a signal that her Filipino identity had been a seasonal tool, something deployed for a press tour and then quietly replaced with a European label when the cameras moved on. The Belonging Engine has a long memory. The community watches both what you claim and what you're willing to walk away from when it's no longer convenient. And the distance between those two things tells them everything they need to know.

The Court as Cultural Territory

The same ownership dynamic that drives the Filipino diaspora's mobilization around global voting platforms is running continuously through the NBA, and it has been for years.

Since 1978, when Raymond Townsend became the first player of Filipino heritage to reach the league, the Filipino community has been watching the NBA with a specific kind of attention. Not just as fans. As stakeholders. As residents who recognized that every time a player with Filipino blood stepped onto that court, something belonging to the community was being represented on one of the most visible stages in American sports.

Jordan Clarkson's grandmother Marcelina Tullao Kingsolver hails from Bacolor, Pampanga. His connection to the Philippines runs deep enough that he became a naturalized player for Gilas Pilipinas, representing the national team at the 2018 Asian Games and the 2023 FIBA World Cup. When he signed with the Utah Jazz in 2019, the team's fanbase in the Philippines grew overnight. His NBA Sixth Man of the Year award in the 2020-21 season was celebrated in the Philippines like a national milestone. That's not brand reach. That's a community claiming an outcome as their own.

Jalen Green's Filipino heritage flows through his mother Bree Purganan, whose grandfather is Filipino. He was the second overall pick in the 2021 Draft, going to the Houston Rockets. In October of that year, when the Rockets hosted the Jazz on Filipino Heritage Night, Clarkson and Green became the first two players of Filipino descent to share an NBA court. The moment was historic by any measure. But what mattered more than the designation was what it meant to the community watching: two Filipino kids on the same floor on the same night, both carrying the frequency, both proving the presence was real and growing.

Dylan Harper's mother Maria Pizarro was born in Bataan, Philippines. She moved to the United States at seven, became a Division I basketball player at the University of New Orleans, and then became her son's first coach, putting him through drills on concrete courts before any national scout knew his name. Her grandfather represented the Philippines in jai alai at the 1968 Summer Olympics. When Dylan was selected second overall by the San Antonio Spurs in the 2025 Draft, cameras cut to Maria in the audience. Her composed presence, her pride, the weight of what she had given her son over decades of concrete-court mornings, went viral within minutes. The community wasn't just celebrating a draft pick. They were celebrating the woman who built him, and the culture she carried into a New Jersey driveway that eventually produced an NBA player. Dylan said it simply: "My mom's side of the family, they've put so much into me."

Dylan's older brother Ron Harper Jr., who shares the same Filipino mother, played for the Toronto Raptors on a two-way contract. Two brothers. The same Filipino mother. Both in the NBA. Jared McCain, now with the Oklahoma City Thunder, acknowledged his Filipino roots during a live stream: "I am a Filipino. I mean, only like 10 percent, but that counts right?" The community's response was immediate and warm, not because ten percent is a large share, but because the community has always understood that the frequency travels regardless of percentage. That counts.

And it extends far beyond the players. Erik Spoelstra, whose mother Elisa Celino was born in San Pablo, Laguna, is the head coach of the Miami Heat and the first Asian American head coach in the history of all four major North American sports leagues. Three NBA championships. Six Finals appearances. Head coach of Team USA. The community has been claiming him since 2008 when he first got the job, long before any institution thought to call it a milestone.

The Field, the Ice, and the Same Frequency

The NFL timeline starts earlier than most people realize. Roman Gabriel, whose father Roman Gabriel Sr. immigrated from the Philippines to North Carolina, was the starting quarterback for the Los Angeles Rams from 1962 to 1972. He was the NFL MVP in 1969, the first and only Asian American ever to win the award. A four-time Pro Bowl selection. One of the most dominant quarterbacks of his era. Playing in Los Angeles, in front of one of the largest Filipino populations in America, the community knew exactly what his presence meant long before anyone in the league thought to schedule a Heritage Night around it. He was the frequency, running through the NFL for over a decade, before the infrastructure to celebrate it existed. He passed away on April 20, 2024, at age 83. The pattern was already written in his career: the community was always already inside these institutions. The institutions just weren't paying attention.

In the NFL today, Cam Bynum made it impossible to miss. The Indianapolis Colts safety, whose mother Jennifer is a third-generation Filipino American from San Francisco with roots in Leyte, walked out of a Minnesota Vikings win over the New York Jets in 2022 with the Philippine flag draped over his shoulders and gave every interview that way. He said it simply: "I rep my roots heavy." He hosts football camps in the Philippines in the off-season, runs a foundation focused on disaster relief and youth empowerment on the islands, and has spent his NFL career making it clear that the flag on his shoulders is not a media moment. It is his actual life.

Josh Jacobs, three-time Pro Bowler and 2022 NFL rushing leader, is one-quarter Filipino through his grandfather, with family roots in Angeles City, Luzon. Nikko Remigio, the Kansas City Chiefs return specialist who helped the Chiefs reach another Super Bowl with a 44-yard punt return in the 2025 AFC Championship Game, carries his Filipino heritage through his father Mark, whose family immigrated from Iloilo and Muntinlupa. Tyler Allgeier, now with the Arizona Cardinals after breaking the Atlanta Falcons' rookie rushing record, has his maternal grandmother's home province of Southern Leyte tattooed on his arm as the Philippine sun and stars. And in the 2026 NFL Draft, cornerback Chris Johnson, whose mother Priscilla Marie Mayo-Johnson is Filipino, was selected 27th overall by the Miami Dolphins out of San Diego State, becoming the latest Filipino American to hear his name called on one of the biggest stages in American sports.

These are not press release moments. They are the way these men carry their identity into their profession every single week.

And the community doesn't wait for the institution to confirm who belongs. When wide receiver CJ Williams was selected 203rd overall by the Jacksonville Jaguars in the 2026 Draft, Filipino flags flooded his Instagram comments within hours. Community accounts amaznhq and socalfilipinos reposted the moment, and Cam Bynum showed up in those comments with four words: "Philippines is boomin lately." Whether or not the heritage claim holds, the community had already decided. That instinct, to find their own and claim them before anyone official says so, is not a marketing behavior. It is Bayanihan running in real time on a draft night feed.

The NHL timeline is longer and quieter, and it starts with Tim Stapleton. Half Filipino, half Irish, undrafted, Stapleton became the first player of Filipino descent to appear in an NHL game when he suited up for the Toronto Maple Leafs in February 2009. He didn't know the historical significance of that moment until years later, when the Robertson brothers arrived and people started getting the timeline wrong. "Someone corrected them," he said. "To this day, the joke is my friends think I called in and corrected them myself." Matt Dumba, the Filipino Canadian defenceman drafted seventh overall by the Minnesota Wild in 2012, became the second. Born in Regina to a Filipino mother and Romanian-German father, Dumba spent his career using his platform as one of the very few players of color in the NHL to push the league toward something more honest about what it was excluding. He co-founded the Hockey Diversity Alliance. He became the first NHL player to kneel for a national anthem. He did both things without apology and without explanation.

Then came Jason and Nick Robertson. Their mother Mercedes was born in Manila and moved to California as a young child. Their father Hugh is Scottish American. The family moved the whole household to Michigan when the boys were young so they could get better access to ice time, a Filipino immigrant mother betting her family's geography on her sons' dream of playing hockey. Jason became the second Filipino American in NHL history and, later, the first Dallas Stars player to record a 100-point season. Nick became the third. Together they became the first siblings of Filipino descent to play in the NHL simultaneously, two brothers in two different arenas carrying the same frequency their mother brought with her from Manila.

And on the football pitch, the community built something that no institution could have manufactured. When the Philippines qualified for its first-ever FIFA Women's World Cup in 2023, eighteen of the twenty-three players on the roster were born in the United States, women of Filipino heritage who chose to represent the country of their parents and grandparents rather than the country of their birth. Goalkeeper Olivia McDaniel, whose mother has roots in Pampanga and Davao, was named player of the match in a historic 1-0 victory over co-host New Zealand. Hali Long, raised in a Filipino household in Missouri, said her decision was simple: "Under our roof, it was purely Pinoy. That's just who I was, without question." The Filipinas didn't wait for the federation to come looking for them in American suburbs and college programs. They found the team. They built the roster. They showed up and beat the co-hosts at their own World Cup.

None of these institutions discovered the Filipino community. The Filipino community has been inside every one of these leagues, on every one of these pitches, watching, claiming, mobilizing, celebrating, and carrying these players forward. By the time Heritage Nights were scheduled and Filipino artists were invited to center court, the community had already decided the outcome. The institution certified what the community already owned.

The Gold Standard: Distributed Ownership

The highest expression of ownership in brand work is what happens when a brand stops trying to be the owner of a cultural moment and starts being the platform through which the community owns it themselves.

The King's Hawaiian Ube Coconut Roll launch is instructive

not because it failed. It didn't. The product is genuinely good, demand has been real and sustained, and the brand took the meaningful step of acknowledging the ingredient's Filipino roots. People in my network reported it selling out immediately. When I finally found it at Costco and Target and tried it, my honest reaction was that I tasted coconut, and when I added butter I tasted butter. I couldn't find the ube. Not really. And that gap between the label and the experience is actually the smaller of the two gaps the rollout left unaddressed.

The bigger gap is this: ube, for me, isn't a flavor I discovered. It's a memory I carry. It's ancestry. It's the round tub of ube ice cream my dad would bring home when I was a kid, the waffle cone at the park on the days he spent with us while my mom was working. It's birthday parties in someone's backyard, the purple dessert that meant celebration and family and being Filipino all at the same time, long before any global brand decided it was a spring trend. King's Hawaiian made ube visible to a wider audience. What it hasn't yet done is make Filipinos feel like it's still theirs.

Distributed Ownership would look different. It would start with timing. April is Filipino Food Month, and the conversation around Filipino food, identity, and culture is already running without any brand having to create it. You don't launch into a trend you manufactured. You step into a moment that already exists. Then you anchor the product inside real Filipino cultural spaces, food festivals, community markets, pop-ups where Filipino food and music and creators already intersect, not with heavy branding or explanatory signage, but with presence. Just there, on the table, the way food is always on the table at a Filipino gathering.

Then you build one core activation around a DJ-led environment. Not a club, not a branded event, not a press moment. A real hang, invite-only or tightly curated, the kind of room where people actually dance and talk and stay. The DJ is not entertainment. The DJ is the creative director of the space, setting the tone, shaping the crowd, defining how everything feels. Inside that environment, the ube rolls are out on the table with everything else. People grab them between sets. They get passed around the way everything gets passed around at a Filipino gathering, naturally, without announcement, because that's how Filipino food has always moved. You capture what actually happens. Real reactions. Real conversations. The small moment where someone puts someone else onto it for the first time. That becomes the content.

From there you expand, a limited capsule tied to Filipino Food Month, a collaboration with a Filipino-owned bakery that already has the community's trust, selective placement at festivals and markets where the same energy exists. The rule stays the same throughout: integrated, never announced.

King's Hawaiian succeeded in making ube visible. The next step, the step that turns visibility into belonging, is showing how it lives rather than explaining what it is. When you stop telling people what ube means and start showing it in the environments where it has always meant something, the product stops being a discovery and starts being a homecoming. That's the difference between a product launch and distributed ownership. And Filipinos will feel which one it is before they've even read the packaging.

From Narrator to Foundation

When ownership is genuinely established, the brand's role transforms in a way that is both profound and, for most marketing teams, deeply counterintuitive. It is no longer the source of all activity, the center of the story, the entity responsible for keeping the relationship alive through constant investment. It becomes something quieter and more durable than any of that. It becomes a foundation, part of the infrastructure the culture builds on rather than the force driving the culture forward.

Without ownership, belonging remains incomplete and entirely dependent on the brand's continued life support. The moment the brand stops investing, the connection starts to fade, because the community was never really carrying it. The brand was carrying it for them. With ownership, that dependency inverts. The community carries the work forward because they have genuinely claimed it as theirs, because it lives in their world in a way that has nothing to do with whether the brand is actively pushing it in any given quarter.

If you aren't willing to let the community change your colors for a night, you'll never be part of their world for a lifetime.

CHAPTER 11

The Autopsy: Why Alignment Fails

—

The architecture of belonging is logically sound in theory. In the boardroom, it is incredibly fragile.

Most efforts to build genuine cultural residency don't fail because the creative was bad or the budget was insufficient or the team wasn't talented enough. They fail because the brand wasn't willing to pay the actual price of entry, the surrender of control, the patience that doesn't fit a quarterly timeline, the willingness to let the community define what success looks like rather than the internal dashboard. Those two things cannot occupy the same space, and culture always wins.

The Gimmick Trap

The most common breakdown happens when a brand confuses doing something with adding something. This is how you end up with a gimmick, an activation that achieves high recognition by mirroring the aesthetics of a community but offers participation that provides zero tangible value. You invite people to a pop-up, give them a photo opportunity, and send them home.

You've asked for their energy and given them nothing to build with. The environment is exactly the same as it was before you arrived, except now the community has a clearer sense of what you were actually there for.

In the Filipino context, this failure often manifests as what I call the *Generic Bucket* error, brands attempting to check a box by lumping the community into a broad Asian category, treating Filipino culture as a subset of a demographic rather than a distinct, specific world with its own Southeast Asian, Pacific Islander, and Austronesian roots that don't belong in the same bucket as East Asian cultures. In the influence model, this works if it generates clicks. In the residency model, it's a total failure because it signals, clearly and immediately, that the brand never did the work of actually understanding who they were trying to reach.

The Trader Joe's autopsy makes this visible in a way that's hard to ignore. The brand leaned into hyper-specific Filipino products, the Ube Mochi Waffle Mix, the visual language of something that felt culturally aware, and then came the Filipino Style Chicken Adobo. The labeling alone tells you everything. By calling it "Filipino Style," the brand inadvertently suggested that there is a standard version and then this corporate approximation of it. And then they translated the dish, adding turmeric and celery seed, softening the sharp, garlicky, vinegary soul of the thing that makes adobo adobo, to make it accessible for a generic palate. In a product development lab, that's optimization. In the neighborhood, it's a tourist order. The community's verdict, that it tastes like bland airplane food, is the audit result delivered plainly. The brand was more concerned with mass appeal than with the sanctity of what they were borrowing.

I looked for that Ube Mochi Waffle Mix everywhere when it launched. It was sold out at every store I checked. I ended up finding it on Amazon at a markup and ordered it because I had to know. When it arrived and I tried it, my honest reaction was: meh. I never bought it again. By the time the Filipino Style Chicken Adobo came out, I didn't need to try it. The community had already run the audit and delivered the verdict, and I trusted the residents over the label. That's not a consumer behavior. That's the belonging system working exactly as it's supposed to. The community's radar was so accurate that it made the product irrelevant to me before I ever tasted it.

This same lack of nuance shows up in how brands consistently misread the history of Filipino music. The Manila Sound has been treated for decades as a localized imitation of Western pop, a derivative rather than an original. But the actual history tells a completely different story. It was shaped by the presence of US military bases, where local Filipino musicians weren't covering American hits so much as refining an entirely distinct fusion of soul, funk, and jazz filtered through Filipino tonality and lived experience. When brands treat Filipino talent as a new trend rather than the latest expression of a century-long dialogue with global genres, they miss an opportunity to contribute to something that was already international before the internet existed.

The Signal Disconnect

Consider what happened with Bruno Mars versus the J.Lo and Shakira Super Bowl halftime show. When J.Lo and Shakira took that stage in 2020, the media, the brands, and the NFL collectively framed it as a definitive cultural milestone for the Latino community, and it was. The cultural significance was named, claimed, and celebrated. Bruno Mars, by any measure one of the most successful artists of the last two decades, has won more

Grammys than almost anyone in his era. His Filipino heritage is not a secret. And yet the industry has consistently declined to frame his success as a milestone for Filipino representation, because his signal doesn't fit the narrow, corporate-defined category of what "Asian" is supposed to look like. His success gets sterilized and filed under general pop, and the community that has been claiming him for years watches the industry look right past what they've always known.

The Coachella history tells the same story at scale. Based on the press coverage of 2026, you might believe that Filipino presence at Coachella began that year. The actual history is that Filipinos have been on that bill since the very first festival in 1999, when DJ QBert and Mix Master Mike provided the rhythmic foundation of the inaugural event. In the decades since, the list of Filipino artists who have performed at Coachella reads like a who's who of artists who shaped the sound of the festival itself: H.E.R., Nicole Scherzinger, Steve Lacy, Dominic Fike, Saweetie, Beabadoobee, Toro y Moi, Eyedress, apl.de.ap, Chad Hugo, P-Lo, Manila Killa, No Rome, Underscores, Yeek, Rhettmatic, Hillari, DJ Gingee, and The Two Lips.

The 2026 festival was genuinely historic. BINI as the first Filipino-based group and first Filipina girl group from the Philippines to perform, bringing the energy of P-pop to that stage with hits like "Pantropiko," alongside KATSEYE led by Sophia Laforteza. Those moments deserved every word written about them. But the framing of those moments as the beginning of Filipino visibility at Coachella inadvertently erases decades of residency that made them possible. When the industry treats a resident as a new guest, it signals that it hasn't been paying attention to the house they've been living in all along. The disconnect isn't just about who gets credit. It's about the refusal to recognize the continuity, the long, unbroken thread of presence that the community has maintained whether or not anyone was writing about it.

The Bahay Kubo controversy involving Filipino-British founder Christina Nadin shows how this signal disconnect plays out even when the person doing the extracting has cultural proximity. Nadin, whose mother is Filipino and who has roots in Bicol, launched bahay kubo as a hair accessories brand in 2024, naming it after the traditional Filipino stilt house. The backlash wasn't triggered by outsiders stealing something. It was triggered by a fundamental value mismatch. In Filipino culture, the Bahay Kubo is the physical symbol of Bayanihan, communal unity, shared labor, the understanding that the community moves together or not at all. When that symbol became the name for a brand headlined by a thirty-five-dollar silk scrunchie, something essential was stripped away. As journalist Kristina Rodulfo noted in her analysis, the core problem was the disconnect between what the name bahay kubo represents and what the product actually delivered, and the founder's failure to respond to the community whose culture the brand claimed to honor. By upcycling the Kubo into a luxury product, the brand made it price-prohibitive and unrecognizable to the people who built it. For the next-generation Filipino community, the signal was unambiguous: this wasn't an invitation to belong. It was a storefront for tourists. Identity is not a hall pass for extraction, and having Filipino heritage doesn't automatically exempt you from the audit.

The Control Tax

The final failure point isn't creative and it isn't strategic. It's legal. True belonging requires a transfer of ownership, the willingness to let the community take what you've built and carry it somewhere you didn't plan for. Most organizations are structurally incapable of doing this because the entire apparatus of brand management is designed to prevent exactly that from happening. I call this the *Control Tax*. If the community can't hack your work, remix it, or carry it forward without a permission slip, they won't. And without that handoff, the relationship remains a permanent, expensive dependency on the brand's constant life support, never self-sustaining, never truly belonging to anyone but the brand itself.

Paradise Rising illustrates this collision clearly. Launched in 2020 as a joint venture between 88rising and Globe Telecom, the label generated real excitement in its first two years, a platform specifically built to bring Filipino artists to a global audience, backed by one of the most credible Asian music brands in the world. By 2022, the releases had slowed significantly. By 2023, the label's last signed artist had moved on. What the surface narrative of a promising launch missed was the structural tension underneath, the challenge of applying a global platform's polish to a market that runs on high-context, grassroots loyalty, in an environment where artistic careers are still too often viewed as hobbies rather than viable, well-funded professions deserving sustained investment. When the ecosystem doesn't get built, when the focus stays on exporting content for a global feed rather than nurturing the local infrastructure that makes artists sustainable, the residents eventually move to independent spaces where they actually own the narrative. The Control Tax was too high, and the community stopped paying it.

The Influence Hangover

Underneath all of these specific failures is the same root cause: a reflexive return to the influence model when the going gets hard. Most brand teams, even the ones who genuinely understand the belonging framework intellectually, reach for the broadcast toolkit the moment they need to show results, because reach is legible, frequency is measurable, and cultural alignment is neither. So the work gets executed at a high production level, the campaign flight runs, the metrics look acceptable, and then it ends. And the impact evaporates with it, because none of the infrastructure of belonging was actually built. Just the appearance of it, maintained for the duration of the spend.

If you aren't willing to stop acting like a broadcaster, you will always be read as an intruder. Not a partner. Not a resident. A landlord who showed up wanting credit for a house they never helped build.

BAYANIHAN 2.0

*The communal
lift, digitized*

In the traditional Western view, community service is an organized, scheduled, and often incentivized activity, a choice made by individuals to contribute to a collective, usually with some form of recognition or reward attached to it. You show up because you signed up, because there's a tax benefit, because it looks good on a resume, or because the company mandated it. The contribution is real, but the motivation is transactional at its core. In Filipino culture, there is an ancient concept that operates on an entirely different logic: Bayanihan.

The classic image of Bayanihan is a group of neighbors literally lifting a house, a bahay kubo, on their shoulders and carrying it to a new location. There is no central authority directing the lift. There is no committee that organized it, no brand that sponsored it, no incentive beyond the understanding that the survival of the neighbor is inextricably linked to the survival of the village. The house moves because the community decides it needs to move, and because everyone inside that community already knows their role without being told. It is belonging-led labor in its most physical, undeniable form.

What most people don't know is how far back the architecture of that belonging actually goes.

The word *barangay*, the small community unit that remains the foundational building block of Filipino society today, comes from the word *balangay*, the name of the outrigger boats that Austronesian ancestors used to navigate the Pacific more than five thousand years ago. Those boats required every person on board to contribute to the journey, from navigation to fishing to rowing to steering, because the survival of the voyage depended on the participation of everyone inside it. They were, in the most literal sense possible, all in the same boat. When those early seafarers arrived and built their communities on land, they named their settlements after the vessels that had carried them, because the logic of the vessel became the logic of the village. The community is not a collection of individuals. It is a crew. And a crew moves together or it does not move at all. That is not a metaphor that was invented later. It is the founding architecture of Filipino communal life, encoded in the language before anyone thought to write it down.

Bayanihan doesn't just describe how Filipinos move houses. It describes how Filipino families are built.

When my parents first came to California, they lived in a house owned by a Filipino family.

That landlord didn't just rent them a room. They helped my parents get established in San Francisco, navigate a new country, find their footing in a place that wasn't built for them. Out of that relationship, when my brother and I were born, that family became our godparents, our *Ninang* and *Ninong*. Their kids became our cousins. We grew up together. There was no transaction that created that bond. There was only the understanding that you help the person next to you, and in doing so, you build something that outlasts any individual act of generosity.

This is why Filipino extended families are so large, so fluid, and so fiercely loyal. The family doesn't end at the bloodline. It expands through every act of mutual support, every moment someone shows up for someone else without being asked. Bayanihan is the reason a landlord can become a godparent. It's the reason the community carries its members the way neighbors once carried houses, not because someone organized the lift, but because that's simply what you do when you belong to each other.

I see this operating in real time everywhere I go. I was recently in Edmonton, Canada for an event, and the front desk staff were all Filipino. The moment they knew I was too, something shifted. They brought me water bottles I would have normally paid for, told me where all the Filipino food spots were in the city, helped me navigate a place I didn't know. Nobody asked them to do that. Nobody was watching. It was just Bayanihan, quiet, instinctive, immediate. The recognition of a shared world expressed through the most practical form of hospitality available to them in that moment.

I find myself acting on the same instinct, especially when it comes to Filipino artists and non-profits. When I see someone from the community trying to build something real, the question isn't whether there's something in it for me. The question is whether I can help carry the house. That's what my parents' landlord modeled for me before I even had a word for it.

My kids get it too, even if they express it in their own way. They'll hear that Bruno Mars is Filipino and immediately say: does that make him our cousin? They're joking. But they're also not. Because in the Bayanihan logic they grew up inside, the answer is closer to yes than no. Shared identity creates kinship. Kinship creates obligation. Obligation creates community. And community, when it's built right, carries everything forward.

Today, that house is no longer made of bamboo. The village is no longer a physical geography. But the logic hasn't changed. It has simply found a new medium. Bayanihan has been digitized. It has become Bayanihan 2.0.

You see it in the way modern Filipino digital communities and diaspora networks mobilize. When a local artist needs support, when a community project needs visibility, when a Filipino creator reaches a platform that wasn't built for them and the community decides that outcome belongs to everyone, the network doesn't wait for a brand call to action. They don't wait for an influencer to give them permission to move. They coordinate with a speed and precision that would bankrupt a traditional marketing agency trying to replicate it, because what's driving the movement isn't a campaign. It's the same thing that drove the original lift: the understanding that what happens to one of us happens to all of us. They are carrying the house through the digital environment.

This is the ultimate proof of ownership, and the ultimate test of whether a brand has genuinely earned its place in a cultural community or is still just visiting. In a campaign-led model, the brand owns the house and the audience is a guest. The brand pays for the maintenance, controls the access, and determines who gets to live inside it.

If the brand stops paying, the house rots, because the community never felt structural responsibility for something that was never really theirs. In a Bayanihan model, the community is the house. And in every meaningful sense, they do.

The shift from 1.0 to 2.0 is the thing most brands fundamentally misunderstand when they try to engage with Filipino culture. Bayanihan is not a marketing tactic you can tap into on a campaign flight. It is not an energy you can rent for a Heritage Month activation. It is a cultural operating system, one that you must earn the right to participate in through genuine contribution, sustained presence, and the willingness to be part of the community before you ever ask anything of it.

If a brand tries to use Bayanihan for its own reach, if it shows up at the lift with a logo and a camera crew rather than a set of hands, the community will drop the house. They will recognize the extraction for what it is, and they will move on without the brand, the way communities have always moved on from people who showed up to document the labor rather than do it.

But if a brand contributes to the strength of the community, if it helps provide the poles that make the lift possible, if it adds something real to the infrastructure that allows the community to carry its own weight, it becomes part of the move. Not the leader of it. Not the sponsor of it. Part of it. And that is the only position worth occupying.

*They are carrying the
house through the
digital environment.*

Compromise in cultural work isn't a middle ground. It's a message.

WHERE BRANDS GO WRONG

The previous section mapped the architecture of belonging, the pillars that support genuine cultural residency and the specific mechanics of how communities recognize, evaluate, and ultimately accept or reject what brands bring into their spaces. The framework is clear. The logic holds. And yet, even when brands genuinely understand it, even when the stated objective is belonging and the team has read the right books and hired the right consultants, the work still fails to take root.

These failures are rarely about talent or resources. The budgets are real. The teams are experienced. The intention, in most cases, is sincere. The issue is something harder to see and harder to fix, the invisible persistence of influence-based thinking operating beneath the surface of a belonging-based strategy. Even when the language has changed, the underlying logic used to make daily decisions often hasn't. What gets approved and what gets cut. How success gets measured. What the legal team will allow and what the brand guidelines protect. All of it remains tethered to the old model, creating a fundamental tension that the community can feel even when the brand cannot.

It is the difference between a DJ who knows the theory and a DJ who knows the room. You can understand every principle in this book intellectually and still walk into a cultural environment and play the wrong record, because knowing the framework and reading the room in real time are two completely different skills, and only one of them actually matters when the music starts.

We are moving from the blueprint of the build to the anatomy of the most common mistakes. And the first one is the most persistent of all.

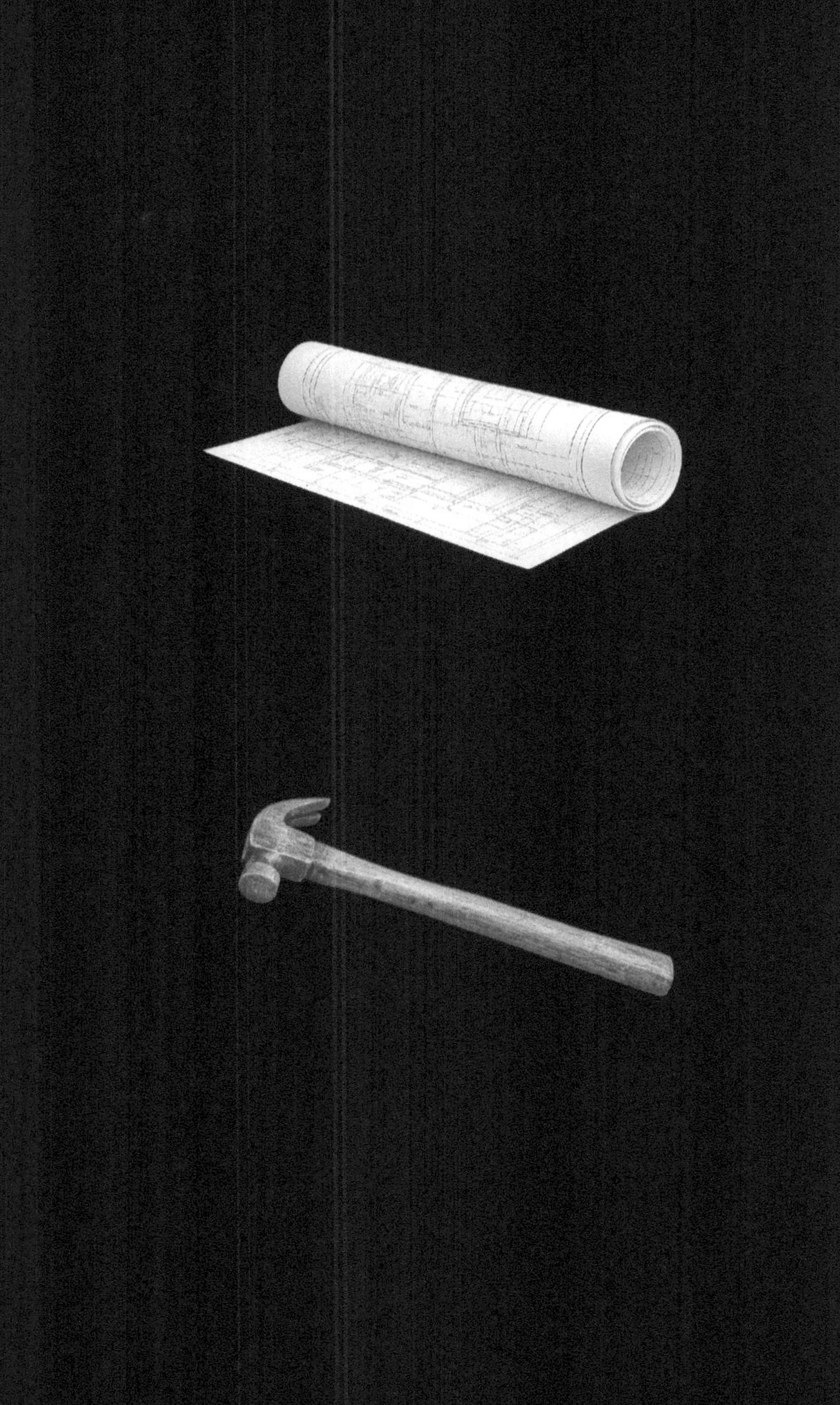

CHAPTER 12

Starting From The Outside

—

Most brand efforts begin from exactly the same position, and that starting position is the problem.

The brand defines an objective. It identifies a target audience. It builds a comprehensive plan to reach that audience, manufactures the creative, selects the partners, maps the distribution, and executes. This process is logical, efficient, and entirely consistent with how influence-driven models are supposed to work, because it starts from the brand and moves outward. When the goal is reach, that sequence makes sense. When the goal is belonging, it creates immediate and often fatal limitations that no amount of execution quality can fix.

The Pressure Test

To understand the weight of this failure, you have to look at what happens when an outside-in strategy collides with the inside reality of the community, the moment I call the Pressure Test.

In the North American market, that collision almost always hits one of three walls: Language, Time, or Category.

The friction around the term *"Filipinx"* is the language wall made visible. The term was built within Western academic and diaspora circles as a tool to address gender inclusivity, an attempt to mirror movements like "Latinx" and create space for non-binary and queer Filipinos who felt the binary structure of certain Tagalog constructions didn't reflect their identity. That was a real and locally specific conversation happening in a specific community. But when brands and institutions picked it up as a broad progressive signal and started applying it across the entire global Filipino population from the top down, they hit a wall of intense and immediate pushback, and the resistance didn't come primarily from conservative traditionalists. It came from Filipinos in the Philippines and across the global diaspora who felt their linguistic soul was being rewritten by people who hadn't done the inside work.

The critics pointed out something the outside brands had entirely missed: the Filipino language is already inherently gender-neutral. *Siya*, the third-person singular pronoun, has never carried a gender. The X wasn't filling a gap. It was imposing a Western framework onto a language that didn't need it, and the letter X doesn't even exist in the original Philippine linguistic system. What the brands read as a progressive software update, the community read as Cultural Imperialism, tourists rearranging the furniture in a house they didn't live in. It was identity rewriting without community ownership, and the community rejected it accordingly.

The time wall shows up in what I call the Nike or H&M model, the brand that appears once a year for Independence Day or Heritage Month with a flag-colored sneaker or a terno-silhouette top and calls it cultural engagement. To the brand, the objective was met. The signal was sent. The box was checked. But the community sees through the simulation with the clarity of people who have been watching this pattern repeat for years. If you are absent from the communal gatherings, the daily rhythms, the unremarkable Tuesday nights that define how this culture actually lives, if you only show up when there's a calendar reason to, the community doesn't read that as engagement. They read it as extraction on a schedule. You aren't a resident. You're a tourist with a recurring calendar reminder.

The category wall is what I call *AAPI Flattening*, the systemic failure of representation through aggregation. When retailers launch AAPI Heritage Month campaigns that lump Filipinos into a broad pan-Asian category, they are making an efficient corporate decision that produces an inaccurate cultural result. The East Asian-coded visuals that dominate those campaigns ignore the specific hybridity of the Filipino diaspora, the Latino influences, the Pacific Islander roots, the American colonial history, the Austronesian foundation, all of the specific threads that make Filipino culture what it actually is rather than what a demographic checkbox suggests it should look like. When a brand ignores all of that and hands the community a generic "Asian" representation, the message received is clear: we see your checkbox, but we don't see your soul.

The Inside-Out Proof

The most definitive proof that environment-first logic wins is the battle between MTV Philippines and MYX, a collision between an outside brand with enormous global weight and an inside brand built entirely from the community's own logic.

MTV arrived in the Philippines with everything the influence model promises: global reach, institutional credibility, a recognizable name that had shaped music culture across dozens of markets. MYX arrived with something different, a genuine understanding of what the environment actually needed. They recognized that the Filipino music community was built around a deep, communal love for Original Pilipino Music, and they leaned into amplifying OPM rather than translating it for a global aesthetic. They integrated videoke culture directly into the viewing experience by displaying lyrics on screen, a feature that seems simple until you understand that it was built from behavioral specificity, from knowing that in Filipino culture, music is not something you watch passively. It is something you do together.

Ryan Cayabyab, the National Artist for Music of the Philippines, understood this better than any institution. He said it plainly: once they play the music and start singing, it makes that community feel that they are home, that they belong. Music has that quality to make the people feel that they are at home. That was not a marketing insight Cayabyab arrived at through research. It was something he had watched happen at every fiesta, every gathering, every room where Filipino music played, across his entire career. MYX built a channel on exactly that truth. MTV relied on global influence. MYX built residency. And eventually, the outside machine couldn't compete with the inside reality.

The MYX origin story makes the logic even sharper. MTV's arrangement with Studio 23 ended, and the network pulled back. MYX launched in its place, not as a replacement for something that had left, but as the channel the environment had actually been waiting for. By the time MYX became a full 24-hour channel in June 2002, its managing director could say something no global brand could credibly claim: OPM and MYX are one and the same. That's not a tagline. That's residency confirmed. The brand and the culture had become indistinguishable from each other, which is the only outcome worth working toward.

I saw the same logic play out in the SF Bay Area Filipino DJ scene, which I didn't discover through a commercial or a marketing campaign. I discovered it in 1989, in my cousin's garage. Two turntables, a mixer, vinyl records, a setup that created a curiosity in me that nothing manufactured could have produced, because it wasn't trying to reach me. It was just alive, and I happened to find it.

Those garages were the original *Silongs*, unclaimed, unbranded spaces where the craft was learned through hands-on discovery rather than a curriculum, where knowledge passed from person to person without anyone asking for permission or credit. The scene that grew out of those garages wasn't just a hobby. It was a sophisticated, self-sustaining ecosystem running two tracks simultaneously, one side throwing parties at clubs and hotels, the other managing weddings and corporate events as a professional business. DJ Showcases in community halls brought six to eight crews together to battle and build their reputations, showing off the latest sound and lighting rigs to an audience that understood exactly what they were watching. The inside voice was constantly advancing itself.

That ecosystem produced DJ Qbert, Mix Master Mike, Shortkut, and Apollo of the Invisibl Skratch Piklz in the Bay Area, and fed directly into the Los Angeles Beat Junkies, D-Styles, DJ Babu, Rhettmatic, and DJ Icy Ice, artists who between them moved from neighborhood showcases to global stages and pioneered turntablism as an art form the entire world eventually recognized. The DMC, the most prestigious international DJ association in the world, eventually asked them to stop competing because their dominance was discouraging other DJs from even entering. DJ Babu said it plainly in the documentary *Scratch*: outside of their parents, DJ Qbert was the only Filipino role model they had. That's not a niche cultural footnote. That's a community building its own infrastructure, developing its own standard of excellence, and producing a global art form from a garage in Daly City.

The same ecosystem that produced world champions also produced Filipino DJs who crossed over into mainstream radio. And it started earlier than most people know. Born in the Philippines, Nes Rodriguez relocated to the United States in 1970. By 1980, DJ Nasty Nes had debuted the West Coast's first ever all-rap radio show, *Freshtracks*, on Seattle's 1250 KFOX. He was nineteen years old. Over the next seventeen years he ran three rap radio shows and helped discover and introduce Sir Mix-A-Lot to a broader audience, co-founding NastyMix Records, which released two platinum albums. Rodriguez later recalled: "I wasn't white, I wasn't Black, they didn't know what I was. Eventually I was starting to let people know that I'm Filipino. All these Filipinos said, 'Finally, I have someone to look up to, who looks like me.' I didn't mean for it to happen, but it happened and it's one of the best gifts that God ever gave me." A Filipino DJ from Seattle built the platform that launched one of hip hop's most iconic artists, decades before any institution thought to celebrate it.

Growing up in the Bay Area, before I ever got into radio myself, I would sit next to the radio and listen to DJ Franzen's mixes, trying to figure out how he was mixing so fast during his 7 o'clock Quick Mix on KMEL. I'd listen over and over until I figured it out, then practice every day to mix like him. What drew me to him wasn't just the skill. It was that he was Filipino and he was on the number one Hip Hop station in the Bay Area. That meant something. I eventually met him years later after high school at a work event I was DJing where he came in as a guest DJ. He started as a fourteen-year-old intern at that same station and eventually co-hosted Snoop Dogg's nationally syndicated show across thirty-five markets before becoming the highest-rated afternoon drive host in Las Vegas. Alongside him were Glenn Aure, who became Music Director at KMEL, and the broader circuit of Filipino radio DJs, DJ Icy Ice, DJ E-Man, DJ Pleez, Rich Laxamana, Majestichris, DJ Melo-D, The Kracker Nuttz, DJ Rich P, and others, the on-air voices that carried the culture into living rooms and car speakers across the diaspora, building a media presence that no brand manufactured and no label funded.

I was part of that world too. I worked at Wild 107.7 which became Wild 94.9 alongside DJ Pleez, Majestichris, and Rich Laxamana in San Francisco, and later made my mark at Z90 in San Diego with DJ Style and DJ Small Wonder. Being inside that ecosystem, seeing firsthand what it meant to have Filipino voices on mainstream radio, and then watching how little of that translated into real visibility for Filipino artists, is what eventually led me to build Heavy Rotation. The station gave me the infrastructure. The gap it couldn't fill gave me the mission.

The YouTube Wave the Industry Missed

The same *inside-out* logic that built the Filipino DJ ecosystem in garages and carried it to global stages repeated itself a decade later, this time through a laptop camera and a YouTube upload button.

In the late 2000s and early 2010s, a wave of Filipino-American artists quietly reshaped the musical landscape without a single major label behind them. Legaci's a cappella cover of Justin Bieber's *"Baby"* racked up 34 million YouTube views and caught Scooter Braun's attention, the group went on to perform on Bieber's My World 2.0 Tour across 300 cities and 30 countries. Melissa Polinar uploaded originals like *"Meant to Be"* and built a global following that earned her a feature at SXSW's first Asian-American showcase and eventually over 84 million streams worldwide. Jeff Bernat's "*Call You Mine*" was placed in the Korean drama *You Are My Destiny* and sparked a devoted fanbase in South Korea, a single moment of lateral alignment that turned into a cross-border career. In 2025, Bernat won his first Grammy Award as a songwriter on DOE's album *Heart of a Human*, the latest chapter in a career that began with a song that crossed an ocean. AJ Rafael built over a million YouTube subscribers and then turned that platform into infrastructure, founding Crazy Talented Asians, a showcase celebrating AAPI performers. Gabe Bondoc built one of the most loyal communities of the era through acoustic originals and consistent fan engagement, proving that connection could outlast algorithmic advantage.

And then there was Jeremy Passion.

His song "*Lemonade*" has passed 120 million Spotify streams. The community across the US, Canada, and the Philippines, without any coordination, without any brand declaring it so, began calling it the Filipino National Anthem. Not because it was the most streamed Filipino song or the most awarded or the most commercially positioned. Because it was the most felt. It traveled the way things travel when belonging is doing the work: from person to person, city to city, diaspora to diaspora, carried by people who heard something in it that the industry never thought to look for.

I wasn't running Heavy Rotation when I first heard Jeremy Passion sing "*Lemonade*." I had stepped away from the music world and was focused on marketing, creative and brand strategy, DJing only occasionally. But hearing his voice did something to me. It pulled at something I had set aside. It made me want to bring Heavy Rotation back. Not because of the numbers, not because of the streams, but because I recognized the frequency. These artists were doing exactly what Heavy Rotation had been built to do: proving that Filipino music was worth a global platform, whether the industry agreed or not.

The industry largely didn't. While these artists were building audiences that crossed oceans and language barriers, the labels were still citing the same Corporate Excuse Framework from the nineties, too niche, not enough data, hard to categorize. Meanwhile, Jeff Bernat had a fanbase in South Korea. Melissa Polinar was performing at SXSW. Legaci was on a world tour. The scale the giants kept saying didn't exist was already there, moving through the culture on its own terms, without a single major marketing budget behind it.

This is the pattern that runs through every chapter of Filipino cultural history, from the garages in Daly City to the radio stations to the YouTube uploads to the Coachella stages. The community builds the infrastructure first. It develops the talent, carries the work, sustains the ecosystem through its own energy and its own loyalty and its own refusal to wait for institutional permission. And then, years later, the institutions arrive and call it a discovery.

It was never a discovery. It was always already there.

The P-Pop Arc

The modern P-pop explosion follows the same arc. While P-pop mirrors the production polish and rigorous training models of K-pop and J-pop on the surface, it is fundamentally an evolution of OPM, tracing its lineage from the 1970s ballads and Pinoy pop through the groups of the nineties and early 2000s like Smokey Mountain and Sexbomb Girls. Groups like SB19 and BINI aren't localized clones of an imported model. They are the export of a specific environment that developed its own voice, skyrocketed through digital integration and viral reach, and built international fanbases by speaking directly to their community through social platforms while keeping their roots planted entirely in the Philippine experience. They moved past visibility toward a distinct voice, and they ensured the story was authored from the inside rather than handed to them from outside.

But residency isn't a static state. It isn't just about living in the house. It's about what happens when the house needs to move. To understand how a community-led system actually travels, we have to look at the logic of the collective lift.

CHAPTER 13

Trying To Influence Instead Of Belong

—

Most brands approach culture with the exact same mindset they use for traditional marketing, and they do it even when they know better. They define a clear objective, build a calculated message, and look for the most efficient distribution channels. Even when the stated intent is deep cultural engagement, the fundamental structure of the work is still built on the mechanics of influencing behavior from the outside, because that's the infrastructure that exists, the process that got approved, the model that the team knows how to execute. The language changes. The underlying logic doesn't.

This creates a persistent, structural conflict. Belonging requires a genuine surrender to the alignment of an environment, a willingness to let the community's reality shape the work rather than the other way around. Influence is built entirely around shaping behavior through external pressure. One is an invitation. The other is an intervention.

Why Jollibee Won

When global giants try to capture the Filipino diaspora, they default to influence through translation, spending millions on localization research to calculate exactly how to Westernize their offering enough to reach non-Filipino Americans without alienating the community they're trying to court. It's an outside-in strategy disguised as cultural intelligence. Jollibee took the opposite approach entirely. They didn't build a marketing strategy for non-Filipinos. They built a residency for the community. They understood that if the inside frequency was strong enough, if the environment felt genuinely, unmistakably like home, the outside world would eventually be drawn to the heat.

They didn't change the sweet spaghetti. They didn't reformulate the Peach Mango Pie. They leaned into the behavioral specificity of the Filipino household and trusted that specificity to do what it has always done: create gravity. It's worth noting that Jollibee's first US store opened in 1998 in Daly City, California, the same community that produced DJ Qbert, the Invisibl Skratch Piklz, and the entire Filipino mobile DJ ecosystem that built its own global standard from a garage. Belonging recognizes belonging. By the time Jollibee became the number one fast-food fried chicken in America, winning USA Today's 10Best award in both 2024 and 2025, beating out Chick-fil-A, Popeyes, and KFC, it wasn't because a clever campaign had influenced the masses. It was because they had provided a *Silong* so authentic that the rest of the world wanted an invitation. Their merch launches and plans to expand to five hundred stores in North America by 2030 aren't marketing stunts. They are the physical growth of a house the community has been carrying for decades, proof that when you build for the resident, the tourist eventually finds their own way to the door.

The Pacquiao Lesson

In the influence model, icons are distribution channels. A brand signs a hero for their reach, borrows their credibility, and hopes the halo transfers to the product. The relationship is transactional by design, protected by morality clauses, and built to last exactly as long as the association produces more value than it costs.

The limitation of this model was made visible in 2016 when Nike severed its eight-year relationship with Manny Pacquiao within twenty-four hours of him expressing his personal religious convictions during a local interview in the Philippines. To Nike, Pacquiao was an influence asset, a way to reach a massive global audience through his athletic dominance. The moment his authentic voice created friction with the brand's global safety guidelines, the asset became a liability, and the transaction was terminated.

The influence was never real. It was a billboard arrangement, and the moment the billboard became inconvenient, both parties discovered they had never actually belonged to each other's worlds. Nike didn't belong to the religious and cultural complexity of Manny's world. Manny didn't belong to Nike's secular corporate structure. They were two separate entities sharing a surface, and when that surface cracked, there was nothing underneath to hold the relationship together.

The Eala Effect

Contrast that with what's happening around Alex Eala, and the difference between influence and belonging becomes impossible to miss.

When fans fill the stands in Madrid or Melbourne to watch Eala compete, they don't come because a brand told them to. They come carrying the rhythm and joy of a Manila street festival into a tennis court, because they recognize a resident. Someone who speaks Tagalog in global interviews when she could easily default to English. Someone who embodies the *sipag* and *disciplina*, the hard work and discipline, that the community recognizes as their own, not as a performance but as the actual texture of how she moves through the world. The community isn't following a call to action. They are carrying the house for someone they believe lives inside it with them.

That's Bayanihan 2.0 in motion. And no media spend manufactured it.

Reading the Room

I've lived this distinction personally every time I travel to DJ in a new city. The influence DJ walks in with a pre-set playlist of Top 40 hits because the data says those are the most impactful songs in the world right now. He tries to force the room to dance to a global template. He has influence data. He does not have the room.

The work of a resident DJ is different. Before I touch a fader in a new city, I study what people are actually vibing to in that specific space. I talk to people on-site. I watch footage of past DJs in that same room to understand the energy that's already been built there, what I think of as the ghosts of the dancefloor. I'm looking for the frequency, and I'm willing to take risks to find it, moving songs in and out, reading the response, adjusting in real time.

I saw the power of this approach at the Lapu Lapu Day Block Party in Vancouver, Canada in 2024. I decided to play VST and Company's "*Awitin Mo at Isasayaw Ko*," a track that in the United States usually gets a polite nod of recognition and not much more. In Vancouver, it blew the roof off. The reaction was electric, especially from the next-generation crowd, in a way I hadn't seen that song land in years. That moment told me everything I needed to know about the specific cultural texture of the Filipino community in Canada, the way certain songs have held their frequency differently across the diaspora depending on where communities settled, how they gathered, what they kept alive. If I had relied on influence data from the US market, I would have missed the heartbeat of that room entirely.

Shifting away from this failure requires changing the starting point. Not: how do we influence this audience? But: how do we align with the environment where this audience already lives? Those are different questions. They produce different work. And the community can tell, in the first thirty seconds, which one you started with.

CHAPTER 14

Borrowing Instead Of Reflecting

—

There is a specific kind of damage that happens when a brand tries to borrow culture. It usually starts in a boardroom with a mood board, someone has noticed a spike in engagement around a specific aesthetic, a trending ingredient, a visual language that's generating numbers, and the instinct is immediate: secure a piece of it before the moment passes. Move fast. Capitalize. The community whose culture is being borrowed from rarely gets a seat in that room, and the decision is made before anyone thinks to ask whether the thing being taken belongs to someone.

In a cultural environment already saturated with this pattern, borrowing is almost always recognized for what it is: extraction. Not engagement. Not celebration. Extraction, the act of taking the fruit of a culture without ever tending to the root.

The Ube Audit

The corporate obsession with ube is the clearest current example of this dynamic playing out at scale. A pantry staple that Filipino families have been cooking with for generations has been repackaged by global chains into a seven-dollar latte, a spring trend, a purple aesthetic moment. The discovery is framed as new. It isn't. The ingredient has been there the whole time, grown, harvested, cooked, and passed down through families who never needed a global brand to tell them what it was worth.

The signal that most brands send when they enter this space tells you everything about their intentions. When a chain can't be bothered to pronounce ube correctly, tripping over "oob" or "oo-bay" while marketing the color to a lifestyle audience, they're communicating something the community hears immediately: they want the aesthetic in the cup and have zero interest in the soul of the people who grew it.

The deeper failure is the refusal to acknowledge the labor. For the Aeta people, one of the oldest Indigenous groups in the Philippines, ube isn't a trend. It's a livelihood, a staple, a thread running through centuries of agricultural practice and cultural identity. Even as US demand has caused exports to explode to over two hundred tons a year, the people doing the actual work of harvesting are seeing a fraction of that value. When a brand uses that ingredient without paying respect to the culinary tradition behind it or the economic reality of the people who sustain it, they aren't celebrating Filipino culture. They are gentrifying it for a quarterly profit, and the community can feel the difference between those two things in the first sip.

The Adobo Autopsy

The same logic of convenience over context is what made the Rachael Ray Filipino Chicken Adobo moment land like a punch in the gut. To understand why the community reacted the way it did, you have to understand what adobo actually is, not as a recipe but as a story.

Long before Spanish colonizers arrived in 1521 and applied the word *adobar* to the technique, indigenous residents of the Philippines were already using vinegar and salt to preserve meat in the tropical heat, a survival method known as *kilawin* or *kilowo*. When Chinese traders later introduced soy sauce, the original white adobo evolved into the version most people recognize today. It is the unofficial national dish of the Philippines not because it's the most elaborate thing in the culinary tradition but because it is the most honest, a blend of indigenous ingenuity, colonial history, and global exchange, carrying all of that in its flavor.

When Rachael Ray stepped into that history, she did it as a tourist with a deadline. She swapped neutral oil for olive oil and *siling labuyo* for jalapeños because they were easier to find, which is the first signal that the culture's soul was negotiable to her. She skipped the marinade. She added vinegar directly to a hot pan. She used measurements like "six turns of the pan" for an ingredient that demands precision and patience. And then she made "garlic rice" with coriander seeds and boiled garlic, producing something clumpy and unrecognizable to anyone who has ever eaten garlic rice in a Filipino home.

The community's reaction wasn't oversensitivity. It was the accurate reading of a signal: this person took the name of something sacred, applied it to something generic, and called it representation. That's what borrowing looks like when there's no respect underneath it.

The Acknowledgment Wave

When reflection works, when the work is built from the inside rather than borrowed from the outside, the difference is felt before it's processed. It doesn't announce itself. It just lands.

The Acknowledgment Wave of 2026 is the clearest demonstration of what happens when residents are finally given the frame rather than just the visibility. Autumn Durald Arkapaw made history as the first woman and the first woman of color to win an Oscar for cinematography, for *Sinners*, a film that required her to hold the visual weight of a story spanning generations and cultures. Autumn is a resident of two worlds, of Filipino and Afro-Creole descent, and her win wasn't borrowed visibility. It was a deeply personal reflection of a heritage that runs from her maternal grandfather's survival of the Bataan Death March all the way to her father's roots in New Orleans. That history was in every frame she composed. You can't borrow that kind of depth. You can only carry it.

The Pitt demonstrates the same principle from a different angle. The show isn't borrowing a Filipino setting for authenticity points. It reflects a documented reality: nearly thirty percent of all immigrant registered nurses in the United States are Filipino. When characters played by Kristin Villanueva, Amielynn Abellera, and Isa Briones speak Tagalog on screen without subtitles, without explanation, without making it a moment, it's not a gimmick. It's the warmth of cultural accuracy that makes a resident reach for their mother's hand and hit rewind. It's the difference between a brand placing a Filipino face in a campaign for a quarter and a project that finally acknowledges the faces that have been doing the work for decades. One is a costume. The other is a *Reflective Residency*, and the community knows which is which before the credits roll.

If you aren't willing to tend the root, you don't deserve the fruit. And the community has been tending that root for a very long time without any help from the brands that now want a piece of the harvest.

CHAPTER 15

Forcing Instead Of Revealing

—

Forcing is a boardroom habit. It happens when a brand studies a map of a neighborhood they've never walked through and decides they want to own the corner. They identify a target community based on demographic data, select a partner based on audience overlap, a statistical ghost with no cultural substance behind it, and then spend significant money on a manifesto designed to convince the public that a relationship exists. The influencer era was built almost entirely on this logic, and it's why that era is dying. When you need a three-paragraph caption to explain why a partnership makes sense, the partnership isn't real. The explanation is the tell. Genuine connection doesn't require a press release.

The Barkada Error

The most instructive clinical study of a forced connection is the 2020 controversy surrounding Barkada Wine Bar in Washington, D.C. The non-Filipino owners chose the Tagalog word *barkada*, meaning a close-knit group of friends, the kind of bond built through years of shared experience and unconditional loyalty, to name their establishment. Their stated logic was a personal association with friendship and a desire to honor a former college roommate. In their minds, they were being appreciative. They had found a word they liked, it resonated with something personal, and they built a concept around it.

What they had actually done was reach into a community they had no relationship with, extract one of its most culturally loaded words, and apply it to a bar that served no Filipino food, employed no Filipino leadership, and had no organic connection to the local Filipino community. *Barkada* isn't a marketing hook. It is a sacred social contract, the specific Filipino understanding of friendship as something deeper than proximity or shared interests, something built through collective survival and mutual accountability. When owners with zero cultural proximity tried to frame their use of the word through a manifesto of college nostalgia, the community's immune system activated immediately. The backlash was intense enough that the owners were forced to change the name before the doors even opened.

That's the cost of trying to purchase cultural warmth without doing the cultural labor. You can't buy belonging with a word you found on the internet.

The Big Three Trap

There is a well-documented friction in the digital Filipino diaspora toward what the community calls brandishing, the practice of reducing an entire culture to a handful of its most recognizable exports and treating those exports as a complete cultural profile. In the Filipino context, this most often manifests as what I call the *Big Three*: Adobo, Lumpia, and Jollibee, deployed as the exclusive cultural currency of every brand that decides it's time to reach the Filipino market.

By collapsing a seven-thousand-island history, a century-long global diaspora, and one of the most complex cultural hybridities on earth into a few takeout containers, brands are forcing a connection through cultural flattening. It is efficient from a production standpoint. It is a total failure from a belonging standpoint. The community recognizes it instantly, not because there's anything wrong with adobo or lumpia or Jollibee, but because they know when those things are being used as a shortcut to avoid doing the actual work of understanding who they are.

The remittance company at the next-gen Filipino concert is the same error in a different category. Their whole identity is built around the first-generation relationship with money, the obligation to send support home, the balikbayan economy. That relationship is real. But it's not the room they walked into. The next-gen Filipino at that event doesn't move money the same way their parents did. I used a remittance service once to send money to a friend who was visiting the Philippines so he could pick up a jacket for me, a piece from a slow-fashion designer doing modern cuts in traditional *Inaul* weave, heritage textiles from the indigenous communities of Mindanao that you simply cannot find outside the Philippines. Totally a non-sales pitch use case. The service worked. But the brand's entire story about who I was and why I was there had nothing to do with my actual life. They were still blindly throwing darts hoping to hit someone, or at least hoping I'd mention them to my parents.

The Barong: Survival Technology vs. Trend Extraction

The forced connection becomes most visible, and most damaging, when it involves objects that carry deep historical weight.

Nowhere is this more apparent than in the way Western institutions have attempted to integrate the *Barong Tagalog*.

In most mainstream fashion contexts, the *Barong* gets treated as a costume or a tuxedo alternative, a sheer, embroidered option for formal occasions that signals cultural awareness without requiring any actual understanding of what the garment is. What those contexts consistently omit is the origin of the *Barong* as a tool of indigenous resistance.

During the Spanish colonial era, the *Barong* is understood to have been designed to be transparent and worn untucked, not as an aesthetic choice but as an imposed dress code, enforced by the colonial ruling class to prevent Filipinos from concealing weapons and to visually distinguish the indios from the colonizers. The garment that was designed to mark subjugation was reclaimed, refined, and transformed into a symbol of Filipino identity and dignity. To a resident, the *Barong* is not formalwear. It is survival technology made of *piña*, pineapple fiber, produced through months of hand-weaving that sustains entire artisanal communities in provinces like Aklan. The labor embedded in a single *Barong* is staggering, and the history embedded in it is irreducible.

When global fashion brands re-label these garments as generic "vintage sheer tops" for a trend cycle, they aren't just missing the context. They are actively stripping the garment of its lineage to make it more consumable for an audience that was never invited into the actual story. The aesthetic gets extracted. The resistance gets erased. And the community is left watching their heritage reduced to a fashion moment that will be forgotten by the next season.

From Forcing to Revealing

The shift from forcing to revealing requires a fundamentally different starting point. Instead of defining a connection in advance, deciding what the partnership means before understanding what the community actually values, you begin by observing the relationships that are already active. You look for the connections that exist without you, the behaviors that run whether or not a camera is rolling, the signals that operate between residents at a frequency tourists can't detect.

When a brand finds a revealed connection rather than forcing one, the entire dynamic changes. The brand stops being a salesman trying to justify its presence and starts being a facilitator of something that was already there. The energy stops going into explaining the relationship and starts going into deepening it. And the community, which has been carrying this culture long before any brand arrived, stops treating the brand as an intruder and starts, slowly and conditionally, treating it as something that might actually belong.

CHAPTER 16

Getting the Room Wrong

—

The most critical decisions about how cultural work gets built are made long before that work ever reaches its intended environment. They are made in rooms, physical and organizational, defined by who is present, how they interpret the information in front of them, and what priorities guide their judgment. Those rooms have their own logic, their own blind spots, and their own definition of what "good" looks like. And when the culture a brand is trying to serve operates under a completely different set of physics than the room that produced the work, the gap between intention and impact can be vast enough to drive a campaign straight into the ground.

The Architectural Vacuum: Love the Philippines

The most complete clinical study of what happens when a room gets it entirely wrong is the 2023 "Love the Philippines" tourism campaign. A top-tier agency and government officials collaborated on a high-budget promotional video intended to showcase the nation's singular beauty to the world. When the video launched, it was quickly revealed that the footage used included stock clips of rice terraces in Bali, sand dunes in the UAE, and landscapes from Switzerland. The agency issued a public apology for the oversight and acknowledged the footage was not original.

This is the ultimate Boardroom Vacuum in action. Within the room, the work looked perfectly aligned because it met the shared internal objective: a generic, high-gloss tropical aesthetic that read as "beautiful destination." The people in that room had a clear goal, a sufficient budget, and a tight deadline, and none of them had enough proximity to the actual Philippines to recognize that the footage they were approving was of somewhere else entirely. They treated the landscape as a skin to be applied rather than a reality to be inhabited, and the result was a campaign that couldn't even identify its own subject.

When you get the room wrong, you don't just miss the nuance. You miss the ground you're standing on.

The Me Room vs. The We Environment

In North America, the default room almost always optimizes for what I call *Me Culture*, designing for a single, individualistic consumer with personal aspirations, personal spending power, and personal reasons for making a purchase. The entire infrastructure of Western marketing is built around this model. The targeting, the messaging, the conversion funnel, all of it assumes a person making a decision for themselves.

The Filipino-American and Filipino-Canadian environments do not operate on this logic. They operate on *Kapwa*, the Filipino concept of a shared inner self, the understanding that the self is not separate from others but fundamentally defined by its relationship to them. This is a *We Culture* in the deepest sense, not as a marketing segment but as a lived philosophy. The actual resident that most North American brands are trying to reach is often simultaneously managing their own financial stability, contributing to the support of an extended household, and factoring in the needs of family members who may be thousands of miles away. The primary driver of spending in this community is not personal aspiration. It is collective security and collective joy.

When a brand optimizes for Personal Status in this environment, they are building for a ghost. This disconnect is why Western brands so consistently misread the Filipino diaspora, they're applying an individualist framework to a collectivist reality and then wondering why the work doesn't connect.

Balut as Spectacle

When a room lacks proximity to the community it's designing for, it will almost always default to treating cultural specificity as either a gimmick or a liability. Nowhere is this more visible, or more damaging, than in the decades-long Western reality TV treatment of *balut*.

For years, shows like Fear Factor have featured balut, the fertilized duck egg that is a genuine culinary staple across the Philippines and much of Southeast Asia, as a gross-out challenge. The format is consistent: present a non-Filipino contestant with the food, film their visceral reaction, engineer the moment for maximum disgust. The room that produces this content is optimizing for spectacle. They have decided that the correct emotional response to this food is horror, and they have built an entire segment around manufacturing that response.

What that room has never stopped to consider is what a Filipino contestant would see. Not a challenge. Not a dare. A meal.

Something eaten at street stalls and family gatherings, something that carries specific memories and specific tastes and specific associations with home. The room that produces the spectacle doesn't know any of that, because the room has never been inside the community it's treating as a prop.

And the cost of that ignorance is not abstract. Every time balut is framed as disgusting on national television, Filipino-American children absorb that framing. They carry it to school in their lunchboxes. They hear it from classmates who have been taught by these programs that Filipino food is something to gag at. A room without proximity will always prioritize the gag over the person's dignity, because it has never had to pay the social price of the joke.

The Perpetual Foreigner

The room's failure to achieve proximity compounds into a psychological architecture that has real consequences for the community. Despite a presence in North America that stretches back centuries, long before most brands knew the community existed, the assumption persists that Filipino Americans are newcomers. The community continues to experience what scholars call the *Perpetual Foreigner* syndrome: the persistent cultural assumption that Filipino Americans are guests in their own country, newcomers rather than residents, foreign rather than native.

Corporate rooms perpetuate this architecture through their defaults. The community gets cast as polite service workers and nurses, visible in supporting roles, invisible in positions of authority, creative leadership, or cultural influence. When brands aggregate the community into a broad Asian bucket, they erase the specific Southeast Asian roots, the Austronesian foundation, the Spanish and American colonial history, and the Pacific Islander connections that make Filipino culture what it actually is. They see a demographic checkbox and design for that, which means they design for no one real.

Getting the room right means seeing the Filipino resident as a permanent, foundational part of the North American landscape, not a newcomer to be introduced, but a contributor who has been building this world for generations and deserves to be treated accordingly.

Activating Residency: The Balikbayan Architecture

The antidote to all of these failures is demonstrated clearly in the Coca-Cola Balikbayan Program in Canada, a case study in what it looks like when a room actually aligns its internal structure with the reality of the diaspora household it's trying to serve.

The program recognized something that most brands miss entirely: the *balikbayan* box isn't a product category or a shipping service. It is a household lifeline, the physical manifestation of how Filipino families maintain connection across the distance that immigration creates. It is filled with specific items chosen over months, assembled with care, and received with a ritual of opening that reactivates the bond between sender and recipient. It is one of the most culturally specific, emotionally loaded objects in the entire diaspora experience.

The program operated through nine Filipino-owned *Sari-Sari* stores across the Greater Toronto Area and partnered with *Atin-Ito*, a community-owned and community-trusted shipping firm. By addressing the rising costs and logistical friction of the *pasalubong* tradition, the deeply embedded cultural practice of bringing gifts to family, the brand didn't try to discover a trend or insert itself into a moment. It made itself genuinely useful within a multi-generational household ritual that was already running. It moved from being a flavor in someone's life to being part of the architecture of how that life functions.

That is what room alignment actually produces. Not a campaign that feels culturally aware, but work that the community actually needed, built by people who understood the room they were designing for well enough to know what was missing from it.

The Resident's Litmus Test

There is a pattern that repeats across almost every failed cultural campaign, and it follows the same timeline. The structure gets built. The strategy gets locked. The creative gets produced. And then, somewhere near the end of the process, someone says: we should probably have a Filipino person check this. A community member gets brought in to review Tagalog spelling, approve a visual, or confirm that nothing is obviously offensive. By that point, it's too late. The foundational decisions have already been made. The architecture is already wrong.

No amount of late-stage cultural consulting can fix the soul of a project that was built from the outside in.

THE DIASPORA SIGNAL

*The communal
lift, digitized*

Traditional belonging is tied to geography. You belong to a neighborhood, a city, a country because you occupy the same physical soil as the people around you, because the infrastructure of daily life, the streets and the storefronts and the faces, creates a shared context that doesn't require explanation. Influence thrives in these fixed locations because it can be targeted through physical infrastructure. You put the billboard where the people are. You buy the local radio spot. You open the storefront in the right zip code.

But the Filipino experience provides the blueprint for something that the old model of reach has no framework for: a culture that learned how to hold itself together across thousands of miles without a singular physical center, and did it so well that it produced one of the most cohesive, mobilized, and culturally specific diaspora communities in the world.

With over ten million Filipinos living outside the Philippines, the culture has had to develop a different kind of infrastructure for belonging, one built not on shared geography but on shared signals. It exists in the Middle Space: the digital threads, the specific aesthetic choices, the coded references that only land for someone who already lives inside the world. And it exists in one of the most tangible, physical, emotionally specific objects the diaspora has produced.

The Balikbayan Logic

The *balikbayan box* is, on the surface, a sturdy cardboard container filled with goods sent by overseas Filipinos to their families back home. To anyone outside the culture, it looks like sea cargo. To the diaspora, it is a physical transmission of signal, a proxy for the sender's presence in a space they cannot physically occupy.

The name itself tells you everything: balikbayan means return to country. The box is the return, compressed into cardboard and shipped across an ocean. What goes inside is never random. The contents, the branded clothes, the specific toiletries, the canned goods that aren't available back home, are selected with precision over months, each item chosen to reinforce a specific connection, to communicate something specific to a specific person about what the sender was thinking of when they packed it. When the box arrives and gets opened, the ritual is celebratorial in a way that has nothing to do with the monetary value of what's inside. It is the reactivation of a shared environment. It is proof that belonging can be shipped, received, and recognized without the two people involved ever sharing the same physical space.

The London Proof

In May 2008, I flew to London to celebrate the one-year anniversary of FilmeFilms, a volunteer-run production company started by second-generation British-born Filipinos to create Filipino-focused content in the UK. The moment I landed and linked up with my affiliates, something became immediately clear: the conversations were the same. The jokes were the same. The cadence was the same. I hadn't adjusted anything about how I was showing up, and I didn't have to.

I spent days before the trip listening to BBC 1Xtra, trying to understand what the London music landscape sounded like so I could read the room when I got there. At the party, it turned out I didn't need any of it. The DJs played the same music we played in the States, the same songs, the same energy, the same instinct for what the room needed, alongside their local sounds. A Filipino artist was painting a mural on the wall. Dance groups were performing. Filipino musicians took the stage. The whole thing was promoted through

Myspace and printed flyers, and the rest traveled by word of mouth. Nobody coordinated the labor. Everyone just showed up and did what needed to be done. Bayanihan, running the same way it runs everywhere.

The only thing that felt different was the accent, specifically, how they teased ours and how we teased theirs. Everything else was the same world. Same cultural nuances: shoes off at the door, *Mano po* to the elders, the specific warmth of a room full of people who don't need to explain themselves to each other. I had dinner at a friend's house where his mother had cooked adobo and bistek, familiar in the way that things from home are always familiar, and slightly different in the way that every household makes it their own. The soul was identical. The seasoning was theirs.

What I observed was a community doing in London in 2008 what the Filipino community in the Bay Area had been doing since the late 1970s, building their own infrastructure when no one built it for them, fighting for the same visibility, amplifying the same music and culture, constructing the same ecosystem of DJs, dance groups, street art, and streetwear. They were about ten years behind the States in terms of where that fight had gotten to, but they were running the exact same playbook. Nobody sent it to them. Nobody franchised it. It was the same culture, traveling on its own signal, replicating itself across ten thousand miles because the frequency was strong enough to hold across any distance.

That's not a marketing outcome. That's a diaspora in motion.

The Signal Is the Location

In the diaspora, belonging is maintained through the signal, not the address.

When a Filipino in London and a Filipino in California and a Filipino in Dubai all react to the same specific cultural nuance, a certain sound, a certain joke, a certain way of navigating a professional environment that only makes sense if you grew up code-switching between two worlds, they are validating their membership in a shared space that has no physical coordinates. The signal is the location. The recognition is the address. And the community that forms around those signals is as real and as durable as any neighborhood built on shared soil.

In 2026, identity has decoupled from geography in ways that affect every community, every subculture, every interest-driven world that people build for themselves online and offline. We live in decentralized environments defined by values and aesthetics and shared references rather than zip codes. These environments are borderless. They do not respond to local marketing because their location is a shared state of mind rather than a physical territory. The tools built for geographic targeting, the billboard, the local spot, the neighborhood storefront, reach the body but not the world the person actually inhabits.

For a brand, the Diaspora Signal represents the ultimate challenge to the old model of reach. You cannot reach a diaspora by buying an ad on a single channel, because the diaspora isn't in a single place. You can only reach it by contributing a signal so accurate, so native, so deeply aligned with the specific frequency the community runs on that the community picks it up and carries it across the network themselves, from London to California to Dubai, without you having to shout in any of those places individually. When the signal is right, the environment is everywhere.

The signal is the location.
The recognition is the address.

Residents adapt. Tourists don't have to, because they're not staying.

BUILDING FROM THE INSIDE

The previous section examined the specific ways that even well-resourced, genuinely intentioned efforts break down. The pattern is consistent across every example. It's never a shortage of budget or talent or production quality that kills the work. It's a fundamental mismatch between the internal structure of what was built and the external logic of the environment it was built for. The room was wrong. The starting point was wrong. The direction of the work was wrong from the beginning, and no amount of execution quality can fix a wrong direction.

A wrong direction can't be fixed with better execution. You can't solve a structural problem with a surface fix. What it requires is a total shift in the direction of the build, not adjusting how the work reaches the community, but changing where the work starts.

Instead of manufacturing something from the outside and then attempting to force its integration after the fact, the process has to begin from within the environment itself. This is not a small change. It fundamentally changes how every subsequent decision gets made, how collaborators are identified and empowered, how information is gathered and weighted, how the work is allowed to breathe and evolve rather than being locked down by brand guidelines and approval chains. It changes who has authority in the room and at what stage of the process. It changes what success looks like and how it gets measured.

We are no longer observing the environment from the outside. We are operating from within it. And that changes everything.

CHAPTER 17

Start With The World, Not The Message

—

Most brand work begins with a message. The brand defines what it wants to communicate, builds a creative concept around that message, and then figures out how to distribute it as efficiently as possible. This sequence is logical within the influence model, because the primary objective is to deliver a crystallized idea to a target audience, and everything else in the process is organized around that delivery. But when the goal is belonging rather than reach, this sequence creates an immediate and often fatal structural ceiling.

Starting with the message assumes that the brand's primary job is to communicate something. It puts top-down control over representation at the center of the process. It treats alignment with the community as a secondary step, a layer of cultural texture applied to a pre-existing corporate brief after the fundamental decisions have already been made. And because the message was never built from inside the environment, the alignment is always cosmetic. The brief is still foreign. The work still moves from the outside in.

The Physics of Timing

For the next-generation Filipino in North America, starting with the world means recognizing something that most Western brand calendars completely miss: the Filipino diaspora operates on its own internal clock, and that clock does not align with the retail cycles that most marketing plans are built around.

This clock is not monolithic. It shifts depending on which side of the border you're on, and once you understand the full shape of it, you realize it never really stops. I tell people half-jokingly that Filipino festival season starts in April with Filipino Food Month, rolls into Asian American Native Hawaiian and Pacific Islander Heritage Month and Philippine Independence Day in June, and then spills into July and August because there are simply too many events to fit into June without overlapping, so organizers push them out. By the time that energy settles, the *Ber Months* have already started in September and the community is building toward Filipino-American History Month in October, with events running across August through October to avoid the same competition. Then it flows directly into *Pasko* and Christmas. That's not a series of disconnected moments. That's a continuous cultural current running from spring through winter. In the United States, the community organizes heavily around Filipino-American History Month in October, the only Asian group in America with its own dedicated history month. In Canada, the environment pivots in June, which is officially recognized as Filipino Heritage Month. A campaign that launches in October might resonate deeply in San Diego and land as a late, disconnected afterthought in Toronto, not because the creative was wrong, but because the timing ignored the specific cultural physics of the environment it was trying to enter.

This timing question reaches its most significant expression in the *Ber Months*, September, October, November, and December, which together constitute the longest Christmas season in the world. The Filipino relationship with Christmas doesn't begin in December. It begins the moment the calendar flips to a month that ends in "-ber," and it builds from there with a momentum that has nothing to do with any retail campaign's launch date. Every household moves at its own pace, some families have been known to put up the Christmas tree in September, others hold off until December, but the psychological and logistical preparation starts early, and it is already well underway by the time most North American brands begin their holiday planning.

By September 1st, the Filipino resident is already calculating the logistics of the season, what needs to be bought, what needs to be shipped, what the *Pasko* gathering will look like, how the budget will stretch to cover everything the collective celebration requires. If a brand waits until November to speak about connection and family and the joy of the holidays, they aren't just late to a retail moment. They are three months late to a conversation that the community has already been having without them. They followed a corporate calendar. The environment was already somewhere else.

I didn't fully understand the *Ber Months* until about five years ago, when working more closely with the community made me realize what I had been missing. I'm a next-generation Filipino who had to rediscover this tradition as an adult. Three years ago I bought a *parol* making kit and tried to teach my kids how to make one. My wife finally agreed to put the Christmas tree up in September. We are building the tradition in real time. Today I'm starting to see *Pasko* events happening in November across North America in ways that weren't there before, a next-generation Filipino community reaching back toward something authentic that the mainstream holiday machine never thought to offer them. No brand put that tradition in front of me. The community did. I found it by getting closer to the world, not by being reached by a campaign. That's the clock running. And it doesn't wait for anyone's media plan to catch up.

The Financial Architecture of the We-World

Starting with the world also means looking at how it solves its own problems, not just what it celebrates, but how it functions at the level of daily economic life.

The Filipino community already has its own sophisticated financial infrastructure, and it doesn't require a bank to run it. The *Paluwagan*, a communal rotating savings association where a group of trusted people pool their money and each member takes a turn receiving the full pot, has been operating in Filipino communities for generations, in the Philippines and across the diaspora. No formal contract. No interest. No institution. Just trust and social accountability, which turns out to be a more durable foundation than most financial products offer. A brand that enters this environment trying to sell a high-interest credit card to build individual credit scores isn't just missing the market. It's misreading the entire financial logic of the world it's trying to enter. The community isn't waiting for a corporate solution to a problem it already solved.

This forensic level of understanding cannot be captured in a demographic PDF or a market research report. It comes from being inside the environment, from watching a next-generation resident in San Diego negotiate a long-distance data plan for their parents, or calculate how to fund the collective holiday celebration while still covering their own rent, or work out the logistics of the balikbayan box alongside their own budget. These micro-moments reveal the true physics of the world: spending is not an act of individual self-expression here. It is a tool for household security. It is an act of collective care. And any brand that designs for the individual without accounting for the collective has designed for a ghost.

Starting with the world is the only path from being a predatory guest to being a valued resident.

Work With People Who Already Belong

—

Environments aren't abstract concepts or data points on a slide. They are living systems held together by the people inside them, the residents who have built the world, who decide what's valuable and what's noise, who determine which behaviors get reinforced and which get quietly rejected. When a brand tries to enter that space, its default instinct is to look for a megaphone, a creator with a massive following who can act as a human distribution channel, a loud voice capable of forcing a message through to the largest possible audience. That's the influence model, and in cultural environments it almost always fails, because what it buys is attention, and attention is not the same thing as trust.

When you're building for belonging, you don't need the loudest voice in the room. You need the *Culture Carrier*.

The Difference Between Reach and Gravity

A Culture Carrier is an artist or creator who doesn't just reflect culture. They move it, shape it, and make people feel like they belong inside it. The distinction between an influencer and a

Culture Carrier is the distinction between attention and gravity. An influencer provides reach and transactions. A Culture Carrier provides trust and identity. When people see something, that's influence. When people feel like they're part of something, that's a Culture Carrier at work. They build worlds with a point of view you can step into rather than a feed you scroll past, and the community doesn't just watch what they do. They participate in it.

The failure of most brand collaborations with creators follows the same pattern. The brand identifies an artist who has the community's trust, someone with real cultural credibility built over years, and then brings them in at the execution stage, when the campaign is already structured and the brief is already locked. The artist becomes a prop, attached to work they had no hand in shaping, used to fix the aesthetic of a foundation that was built by tourists from the beginning. The community can feel the seam immediately. The collaboration produces neither the cultural resonance the brand was hoping for nor the creative integrity the artist has spent their career building.

The best Culture Carriers don't fit into campaigns. They co-create them. They move culture naturally because they are culture in motion, and the only way to work with them honestly is to involve them when the ink is still wet, before the brief is locked, before the concept is final, before the brand guidelines have been applied to everything. It requires a genuine surrender of the ego that most brand custodians are hired to protect. You have to allow the Culture Carrier to co-create the soul of the project, the framing, the interactions, the tone, the technical standards. Real alignment happens when the brand allows the resident to dictate the vibe rather than the other way around.

Sony and the Professional Standard

The clearest current example of this done right is Sony Electronics and their selection of Filipino-American Audio Ambassadors, Brian Puspos, DJ Lex, and Ian Asher.

On paper, these are brand ambassadors. In practice, Sony has anchored its products to residents who define the professional standards of the environments those products live in. Brian Puspos is a choreographer, dancer, and singer whose work is learned and recreated by communities globally. He doesn't show headphones, he integrates them into the technical process of a creative practice that demands sonic precision at a level most consumers never experience. DJ Lex brings the gear into her daily life, the LinkBuds, the WH-1000XM6 headphones, integrated naturally into her world rather than staged in a professional setting. The signal isn't "this DJ uses this equipment on the job." It's something more intimate than that: this is how she actually moves through her day, and the product moves with her. For her audience, that's more persuasive than any booth validation, because it doesn't feel like validation at all. It feels like proximity to someone they trust. Ian Asher is a DJ and producer who represents what he calls sound-flip culture, turning everyday audio into viral sonic experiences that his audience then uses to build their own worlds.

For these creators, Sony's gear isn't a lifestyle accessory. It is a native tool in a high-resolution technical environment where the work itself is the proof. By anchoring the brand to these residents rather than hiring influencers to post photos of the product, Sony stops selling audio and starts participating in the professional standards of the creators themselves. The community doesn't see a brand endorsement. They see the tools that the people they trust actually use. That's a completely different signal.

The Knorr Standard

The Knorr x AJ Rafael partnership for Chili Liquid Seasoning demonstrates the same principle from a completely different angle, and shows what happens when a brand is willing to fully surrender the creative to the Culture Carrier.

Instead of a stiff corporate commercial, AJ and Alyssa Rafael built a world around a karaoke-style jingle, *Pop, Patak, Ang Sarap!*, that earned 5.6 million views on Instagram. But the view count is the least interesting metric in the story. The real proof was in the comments. Residents didn't respond like consumers who had been marketed to. They responded like participants who had been invited into something. They tagged friends. They validated the Pop ritual. They engaged with the karaoke energy, the presence of Sisig, the Boodle Fight, the specific Filipino domestic world that AJ and Alyssa brought to the frame. The brand had given them a world to live inside, not a product to evaluate.

What made this work was a moment early in the creative process where the brand proposed a more upbeat direction, something sticky and designed to lodge itself in memory, and referenced an existing jingle as the target feel. The brand also asked, in the same round of notes, that the Filipino flag be removed from the video treatment. Both instincts came from the same place: a preference for what felt safe and broadly legible over what felt specific and true. AJ pushed back, shifting the tone toward something fun and tropical and communal. The brand listened.

By allowing the Culture Carrier to dictate the vibe rather than execute a predetermined brief, Knorr moved from being a guest in the kitchen to being a resident at the table. That's not a subtle distinction. It's the whole game.

CHAPTER 19

Design Participation, Not Campaigns

—

Most brand work is structured as a campaign, a surgically defined objective with a rigid timeline, a finite set of deliverables, and a media spend that runs for a predetermined window before the whole thing stops. This structure is designed to broadcast a specific message and manufacture a burst of attention. Nobody builds a home in a pop-up.

Designing for participation requires something different. Not an execution plan but a creative system, one that shifts the focus from what the brand wants to say to how people can actually take part in the environment being built. Participation doesn't just happen because the creative is good. It has to be engineered, through a specific architecture of Access, Roles, and Interaction. Get all three right and the system sustains itself. Get any one of them wrong and the whole thing collapses back into a campaign the moment the budget runs out.

Access and the Friction Paradox

The first design challenge is access, and it comes with a paradox that most brands get backwards. The instinct is to remove all friction, to make the entry point as smooth and frictionless as possible so that the maximum number of people can participate with the minimum amount of resistance. But in a high-context cultural environment, frictionless access can actually signal the wrong thing. It can feel like a marketing funnel rather than an invitation into a world.

The real goal isn't to remove friction. It's to align with the friction that already exists inside the culture, to build an entry point that feels native to the environment rather than engineered for it. If you have to explain the call to action, you've already failed to respect the world you're entering. In a high-context environment, the community should be able to feel immediately how they belong inside what you've built, without instruction.

The clearest example of this principle working at scale is Seafood City, and specifically, what the brand has built with *Late Night Madness*.

The origin story matters as much as the event itself. It didn't start with a marketing brief. Seafood City's Director of Digital Marketing and Events Patricia Francisco had been developing the concept after watching coffee shops bring in DJs during the day. Around the same time, DJ JP Breganza, known for playing unconventional venues like rest stops and salt flats, tagged Seafood City in an Instagram post offering to play a set. Francisco recognized what was happening and said yes. After Breganza posted videos from his first set in September, he and the store went viral, prompting a flood of comments asking for more events and requesting he play at other locations. Francisco didn't manufacture a campaign from scratch. She amplified something organic that the community had already validated. That decision changed everything.

CAKES BREADS PASTRIES CAKES BR
Seventy-six nights.
No paid media.
Full rooms.

From September through December 2025 alone, Seafood City ran 76 *Late Night Madness* events across California, Las Vegas, Seattle, and five Canadian cities, without paid media driving the attendance. That's not a campaign metric. That's gravity.

On paper, it's a grocery store. In practice, it has become one of the most talked-about Filipino cultural experiences of the year. These late-night events turn the store, by the meat and fish section, under fluorescent lights, into something that feels like a garage party scaled to a music festival. Filipino DJs spinning party bangers, OPM classics, remixes and today's hits. Fish balls and *qwek qwek*. Datu Puti vinegar shots in Eagle Rock, Mamasita's sinigang mix shots in Toronto, a DJ getting lifted in a shopping cart in Daly City. Crowds doing *Todo Todo* line dances close to midnight, grandparents and grandkids side by side on the same floor, the older generation teaching the moves and the younger generation making them their own, then turning around and jumping to West Coast R&B while the uncles nod along from the food court tables.

I brought my entire family to these events, my in-laws, everyone. In Daly City I saw people I hadn't seen since high school. In San Diego I ran into coworkers from my radio days. There were non-Filipinos there too, fully vibing, not standing on the sidelines, couples who showed up not knowing what to expect and stayed because the energy was undeniable. DJ JP Breganza described it simply: "The fact that I was able to play for four different generations of Filipinos within one room and cater to them all was so beautiful to see." Each city had the same energy but a completely different flavor, because the DJs read their specific rooms and the communities brought their specific selves.

Stephanie Ramos, Co-Founder of Baryo Entertainment, one of the creative forces behind some of these events, put it plainly:

"Filipino-American DJs have been quietly influencing the sound of global music for decades. *Late Night Madness* puts them front and center, not just as entertainment, but as cultural leaders. Seeing them control the energy of a room inside a Filipino space is powerful."

This is not a marketing activation. Seafood City didn't impose a campaign on the community. They gave the community the mic, the music, and the space, and then got out of the way. The result is a recurring ritual that doesn't need promotion to fill rooms because it's already aligned with behaviors that exist independently of any brand objective. The RSVP isn't a data-mining tool. It's a digital velvet rope for a garage party at scale.

What looks like a retail environment is, in practice, a cultural infrastructure, a space that organizes behavior around gathering rather than transaction.

The Necessity of Roles

Once people are inside the environment, the depth of their involvement depends entirely on whether there are meaningful roles available to them. Without roles, participation collapses into passive consumption, people looking at something rather than being part of it. The roles don't need to be complex. They need to be significant. People need to understand, intuitively and without instruction, how they can engage and what their involvement actually contributes to the whole.

The most elegant expression of this principle in Filipino culture is karaoke, not as an activity but as an environment. The structure is minimal. The roles are precise and universally understood: the singer occupies the spotlight, the next-up prepares at the edge of the room, the hype crew reacts and rotates in with a specific energy that everyone knows how to read. No instructions are given because none are needed. The system is entirely lateral, driven by shared energy and accumulated familiarity, and it sustains itself across generations without any promotion because it is built around behavior that already exists in the community.

Any participatory system that fails to achieve this kind of intuitive role clarity isn't lacking creativity. It is misaligned with behavior. The roles aren't designed well enough for people to find them on their own, which means the system will always require external energy to keep running, and the moment that energy stops, so does the participation.

Lateral Interaction

The third layer is the one most brands skip entirely, which is why most brand communities never become actual communities. True participation isn't just about individual actions directed at a brand, a comment, a vote, a share, a tagged photo. It's about how those individual actions connect people to each other. That lateral connection is the moment a project stops being a campaign and becomes something people genuinely inhabit.

The failure of most heritage campaigns isn't in the content. It's in the sequence. The ask comes before the belonging. The brand builds a platform, asks for engagement, and then discovers that engagement without a lateral interaction layer is just a one-way transaction with extra steps. They've flattened a community's identity into a playlist instead of a place, and there's nowhere for the participant to actually go once they've clicked.

Undiscovered SF is the mechanical proof of what lateral interaction looks like when it's engineered correctly. Built as an incubating tool for the SOMA Pilipinas cultural district in San

Francisco, the system creates an ecosystem where artists, vendors, and DJs interact in ways that force a repeatable ritual, not because anyone is told to participate, but because the design of the space makes connection the natural behavior. Attendees don't just show up. They pull up, eat, network, discover, and return, and the system has moved vendors from pop-up tables into permanent brick-and-mortar locations because the interaction layer was strong enough to sustain real economic activity. Over $1.3 million in sales, generated not through top-down broadcasting but through the compounding effect of lateral connection designed into the environment from the beginning.

Measuring Gravity

This shift in design requires a corresponding shift in how success gets measured. A campaign is evaluated within a defined, artificial window, impressions, clicks, engagement rate, conversion, all measured against the performance targets set before the work launched. These metrics are built to assess broadcast effectiveness. They have almost nothing to tell you about whether belonging is being built.

Participation is evaluated through gravity, the degree to which activity continues, deepens, and evolves after the active investment ends. The questions that matter are different: Is the community still talking about this when there's no media spend behind it? Are people returning without being prompted? Is the behavior sustaining itself through the off-season, when no campaign is running and no one is watching the dashboard?

If a system needs constant promotion to stay alive, it was never built for participation. It was built for attention, which is a different thing entirely and considerably cheaper to measure.

The proof of a participation-first system isn't in the performance window. It's in what happens when the window closes and the community keeps moving anyway, because the environment you built gave them somewhere real to live.

Seafood City didn't build a campaign. They built a place. And the community moved in.

CHAPTER 20

Stay Long Enough To Matter

—

Participation creates involvement. Contribution adds value. Signals establish alignment. Together these elements allow a brand to enter a cultural environment and function within it, to be present, to be recognized, to begin the work of belonging. But none of them determine whether that presence is ultimately respected or merely tolerated. That determination belongs to Continuity alone. Without it, everything else eventually collapses into a memory the community files under "brands that showed up once."

The vast majority of brand efforts are structurally incapable of staying long enough to matter, because they are designed to solve an internal problem rather than a cultural one. They are engineered to produce a spike in results within a surgically defined timeframe, the quarterly campaign, the Heritage Month activation, the fiscal-year initiative with a start date and an end date and a set of KPIs that get evaluated and archived. Activity reaches a fever pitch. Performance is measured. The internal objective is met. Resources get reallocated to the next priority. And the community, which was just beginning to form an impression of whether this brand might actually mean something to them, watches it disappear.

In the world of belonging, leaving too soon is indistinguishable from never having been there at all.

The Conflict of Cycles

True continuity requires something that most brand calendars are not built to accommodate: a shift from intensity to rhythm. The burst model, loud for thirty days, invisible for the next ninety, is not just ineffective in cultural environments. It is actively hostile to the kind of integration that belonging requires.

The Festival of Philippine Arts and Culture, FPAC, is the clearest demonstration of what rhythm produces over time. Its significance to the Filipino community isn't tied to any single standout year or particularly spectacular edition. It is tied to the fact that it keeps coming back. Each return reinforces its place in the community's calendar. Each iteration builds on the one before, deepening the expectation that this thing will happen again, that it can be planned around, that it is part of the infrastructure of Filipino cultural life in Southern California rather than just an event that happened once and might happen again. Artists build around it. Vendors depend on it. The community anticipates it the way they anticipate the things that have always been there. Its relevance is not driven by intensity. It is driven by duration, the compounding weight of showing up, year after year, in a way that fits the environment.

That is what rhythm produces. Not a viral moment. A place in the constellation.

Reliability as a Generator of Trust

Consistency is the only true generator of cultural trust, and it works through a mechanism that is simple to understand and genuinely difficult to execute: repetition within the environment's own logic, sustained long enough that the community stops evaluating your presence and starts expecting it.

This is why Filipino family gatherings require no formal promotion. They happen because they always have. The expectation of their return is baked into the structure of family life, into the rhythms of the household, into the way the calendar is read. Nobody sends a save-the-date for *Noche Buena*. Nobody promotes the next birthday party. These things happen because they are part of the architecture of the world, and their return is what gives them meaning rather than their novelty.

The Signal of Absence

Maintaining this presence requires a discipline that most brand organizations are not designed to sustain, the discipline to keep showing up when there is nothing measurable to show for it. When the dashboard is quiet. When there's no launch to justify the spend. When the Heritage Month is over and the next shiny object is already competing for the budget.

This is exactly where most efforts fail. A brand can enter a cultural moment with genuinely good intent and genuinely appropriate creative and still collapse into irrelevance, not because the work was wrong, but because there was nothing after it. The community registered the presence. They noted it. They formed the beginning of an impression. And then the brand disappeared, and the absence became the defining signal, louder, ultimately, than anything the campaign had said.

When the initial win gets recorded and the budget moves on, the relationship gets severed before it ever had a chance to take root. The community doesn't carry a brand that left. They carry the brands that stayed, because staying is the proof that the relationship was ever real.

The Institutional Pattern

I've watched it happen firsthand. An institution sees the energy of something like *Late Night Madness*, witnesses the community responding at a level their own campaigns never produced, and immediately pivots to ask how they can replicate it for their own next-gen strategy. The answer, of course, is that you can't replicate what you didn't build. The community already knows who was in the room before it mattered and who showed up after it was safe.

This pattern repeats across industries and across decades. The institution waits. It watches someone else do the hard work of earning residency. It sees the community respond with a loyalty and an energy that no paid campaign ever generated. And then it arrives, late, underprepared, and wondering why the community doesn't treat it with the same warmth it showed the brand that built the house. The answer is always the same: the community knows the difference between someone who showed up to help build and someone who showed up to move in after the construction was done. And they remember which one you were long after you've forgotten which one they wanted.

Remaining in the Room

Staying long enough to matter doesn't guarantee belonging. Nothing guarantees it. But it creates the only possible conditions under which belonging can develop, because belonging is not a moment, it is an accumulation. It is the weight of return, layered over time, until the presence stops being something the community evaluates and becomes something they simply expect to find when they look up.

When that shift happens, the brand's role in the environment transforms. It stops being an external participant that shows up with objectives and leaves when they're met. It starts being a native part of the ongoing activity of the space, part of the furniture, part of the rhythm, part of the constellation that the community navigates by.

That shift is slow. It is gradual. It cannot be rushed or manufactured or compressed into a campaign timeline. It depends entirely on one thing: the brand's willingness to simply remain in the room, doing the work, after the metrics have stopped proving it's worthwhile and before the community has started to trust that it's real.

And for the Filipino community, return has never required a ticket home.

Identity has changed the standard by which brands are judged. It has shifted the question from what is being said to whether it fits.

THE SHIFT AHEAD

Everything in the previous sections has been about mechanics, the specific, structural ways belonging gets built, maintained, and broken. The pillars. The patterns. The autopsies. The blueprints. All of it has been operating at the level of the individual interaction, the specific brand partnership, the particular campaign that succeeded or failed and why. That level of granularity matters. You can't build for belonging without understanding the mechanics of how it actually works.

But mechanics alone don't explain why this shift is happening now, or why it's permanent rather than cyclical. The shift from influence to belonging isn't a trend in marketing execution or a new framework that will be replaced in three years. It is a response to a fundamental transformation in how people form their identities, how they organize their worlds, and how they decide what deserves their trust and attention.

We are moving away from a world of centralized, mass-distributed influence, where a small number of institutions controlled the channels and the audience's primary role was to receive, and into a landscape that is fragmented, decentralized, and defined by deep, localized belonging. The traditional levers of reach and frequency are not just less effective. They are becoming actively counterproductive in the environments that matter most.

This is the shift from speaking at the world to being an indispensable part of it. And the brands that understand this shift now will not just survive the next decade of cultural transformation. They will be carried through it by the communities they chose to build with rather than broadcast at.

CHAPTER 21

Identity Changes The Standard

—

The role of brands has transformed fundamentally alongside the evolving role of identity in human life, and the two shifts are not coincidental. They are the same shift, seen from different angles.

In earlier models, brands were evaluated primarily on function and utility. People chose products based on a pragmatic calculation: price, availability, performance, and whether the thing did what it claimed to do. That model still exists. But it no longer explains the logic behind how most decisions that actually matter get made.

Identity now plays the dominant role. People don't just use products anymore. They use them to construct and broadcast a sense of self. The affiliations they choose, the objects they carry, the brands they're seen with, all of it has become part of how people communicate who they are and where they belong. These choices are not primarily about what a thing does. They are about what it means, what world it comes from, and whether it fits within the broader context of the life the person is building. Because of this, the standard for engagement has shifted from the objective to the subjective, from does it work to does it fit, and fit is an entirely different kind of evaluation that persuasion cannot override.

The Standard of Fit

When identity is involved in a decision, the evaluation process changes in ways that most marketing frameworks aren't built to account for. People stop asking whether something performs adequately and start asking whether it aligns with who they are and how they want to be perceived by the people whose perception matters to them. In this landscape, fit is infinitely more important than persuasion, because persuasion operates on logic, and identity operates on recognition.

The mechanical reality of Jollibee in North America illustrates this distinction more clearly than almost any other example. From a purely functional standpoint, the decision to choose Jollibee over faster, cheaper, or more convenient alternatives cannot be justified through optimization. There are objectively easier options for every meal the brand serves. And yet it remains a consistent point of cultural gravity, lines around the block for new openings, social media content generated voluntarily by the community, an emotional relationship with the brand that no amount of advertising could manufacture.

That's what identity-driven belonging produces: a brand that doesn't compete, because the community has already decided it belongs.

Signal Fidelity: Overt and Subtle

A product can meet every functional requirement and still be rejected if it doesn't align with the user's identity. Conversely, an object can have minimal utility and immense value if it carries the right signal at the right frequency. These signals operate across a spectrum, from overt declaration to subtle recognition, and the Filipino creative community has been building along that entire spectrum with a sophistication that most institutional brands still can't read.

On the overt end, brands like Illa Manila, Kampeon, and Sunkissed Pinay provide clear, recognizable markers of belonging, Tagalog phrases, athletic heritage silhouettes, a shared aesthetic of the Pinay experience that broadcasts identity loudly and intentionally. They are designed to be immediately legible to the community and largely invisible to everyone outside it. The signal is the point. The recognition it produces is the product.

But the standard has also evolved into a space of what I call *Subtle Signal Fidelity*, brands that have moved beyond overt cultural declaration into something more refined and more demanding. Monday Suck, Abakada, Bago, and Isla Project don't need to announce their identity. They communicate it through specific silhouettes, curated palettes, and community-driven drops that function as a mirror for their audience rather than a billboard. Abakada's subtle "+63" references. Monday Suck's commitment to timeless essentials. The slow-fashion ethos of Abaka, the barbering-lifestyle blend of Sago Studio, the aspirational global cool of Nostalgia. None of these brands are shouting. All of them are deeply, precisely understood by the people they're built for.

In these systems, the value is not in the fabric or the product spec. It is entirely in the signal, the specific, accurate frequency that tells the right person: this was made for the world you live in.

Fluency vs. Recognition

This shift extends to language itself. The use of *Taglish*, the natural code-switching between Tagalog and English that characterizes how many Filipino Americans and Filipino Canadians actually speak, is not a linguistic compromise or an efficiency failure. It is a behavioral identity marker. It is not the purest form of either language. It is the most accurate reflection of a lived reality that occupies the space between two worlds, and it signals something that neither language can signal alone: I am from the same middle space you're from. I navigate the same two operating systems you do. I know what that feels like.

Fluency is not the goal in these moments. Recognition is. And recognition is a completely different register than persuasion.

Influence is notoriously ineffective under these conditions because persuasion operates on logic and identity operates on fit, and no amount of logical argument can close a fit gap. If a brand doesn't natively belong within the identity framework of an environment, increasing the volume of the message doesn't help. It makes the mismatch more visible and more annoying. In cultural environments where identity is at stake, misalignment is not quietly ignored. It is noticed, called out, joked about, and passed around. The community doesn't debate whether it works. It recognizes that it doesn't belong, and it moves on.

None of this changes the entry requirements. Products still need to perform. Services still need to deliver. Every creative decision still needs a why that holds up to scrutiny, a quality of craft that earns the right to be in the conversation at all. But performance alone is no longer a sufficient defense. It is the entry fee, not the winning condition. The brands that have understood this have stopped trying to persuade their audience and started trying to align with their identity, to understand how people define themselves within specific environments, and to figure out how the brand can honestly and sustainably inhabit that same space.

In the world of belonging, people don't choose the best option. They choose the right one.

CHAPTER 22

Culture Is The System

—

Identity shapes how people see themselves. Culture is the invisible system they operate within, and the distinction between those two things matters more than most brand strategies account for. *Identity is the mirror. Culture is the machine.*

In the traditional marketing world, culture gets treated as a surface layer, a collection of trends, viral moments, and aesthetic expressions that brands can tap into by aligning with whatever is most visible at any given moment. This view is functionally incomplete in a way that produces consistent, predictable failure. When you treat culture as a surface, you engage with the output without understanding the underlying structure that determines what gets produced, what gets kept, and what gets quietly rejected. Culture is not a trend layer. It is a comprehensive operating system, one that defines the fundamental laws of how people in a specific environment interact, which behaviors get reinforced and which get sanctioned, and how value moves through the community. It is the machine that determines not just what is visible but what is allowed to become visible in the first place.

The Logic of the Environment

Within any cultural system, variables do not carry equal weight. Some signals get decoded instantly and carried forward. Others get filtered out as noise before they've had a chance to land. Every cultural environment has its own standard, a set of unspoken rules that govern the pace, the tone, and the etiquette of participation. These rules are never written down. They don't need to be. They are enforced with absolute consistency by the residents through the most powerful regulatory mechanism available: repetition and absence. What fits keeps showing up. What doesn't simply stops appearing.

Filipino potluck culture is one of the clearest expressions of this system I know. What gets brought to the table follows a specific cultural logic that no one has ever formally articulated but everyone inside the culture understands completely. Certain dishes are expected, their presence is so reliable that their absence would be noticed and remarked upon. Others disappear quietly after one appearance, not because anyone said anything, but because the system communicated its verdict through silence. No one explains the standard. The behavior teaches it. Work that aligns gets carried forward. Work that doesn't simply doesn't come back.

The same instinct shows up in the most unexpected places. On Royal Caribbean cruises, Filipino crew members are often responsible for encouraging passengers to wash their hands before entering the buffet. What could have been a rote public health announcement became something else entirely, a performance, a jingle, a moment of communal joy delivered with complete commitment: *"Washy Washy before Yummy Yummy."* When I first heard it I laughed, and then I thought: only Filipinos could take an instruction like that and turn it into something people actually enjoy. Not because it was assigned to them. Because that's the system running. The culture found the communal angle in a hand-washing reminder on a cruise ship, made it performative and warm, and turned a transaction into a moment of connection. That's not a campaign. That's a cultural operating system expressing itself through whatever container it happens to be in.

This is culture as a living regulatory system, operating below the level of conscious decision-making, enforcing its own standards with a consistency that no brand guideline has ever achieved.

The Gatekeeper's Toll

Understanding culture as a system changes how you measure success. In the broadcast model, success is measured by reach, how many people were exposed to the message within the campaign window. In a system-based model, success is measured by integration, how well the work continues to function within the environment after the brand has stopped actively pushing it. Not whether it performed during the flight. Whether it survived past the flight, and what it became inside the community once the brand was no longer driving it.

In this landscape, audiences have stopped being passive recipients and become active gatekeepers. They are not evaluating whether your work is good in an abstract sense. They are determining whether it belongs inside their world, whether it fits the lived-in logic of the environment well enough to be adopted, carried forward, and woven into the daily rituals of the people inside it. Work that passes this test gets integrated. Work that doesn't isn't just ignored. It gets identified as an imposter and rejected with a clarity that the brand often can't even see coming, because the rejection happens in private group chats and around dinner tables rather than in public comment sections.

Integration and Autonomy

Integration is a gradual process, and it produces something that most brand strategies are never designed to achieve: Autonomy, the stage where the work no longer depends on the brand to keep it alive.

In the influence model, the brand is the engine of everything. The message exists because the brand is spending money to keep it in circulation, and the moment that spend stops, the message disappears. The relationship between the brand and its visibility is direct and entirely dependent. In a system-led model, the participants within the environment become the engine. They decide collectively whether the work is worth adopting, adapting, or extending. They take the creative decision and weave it into their own daily rituals, their own private conversations, their own ongoing construction of what the world they live in looks, sounds, and feels like. The brand's role shifts from source to seed, and once a seed takes root in the right environment, the environment does the growing.

This is the true nature of belonging when it's working correctly. It is not an isolated marketing outcome. It is the natural result of alignment within a cultural structure, the brand and the community operating at the same frequency for long enough that the distinction between them begins to blur in the best possible way.

Because culture is a living system, this alignment requires ongoing observation and ongoing adjustment. The community evolves. The environment shifts. What fit perfectly a year ago may need to be recalibrated. This is not a problem. It is the nature of being genuinely inside a living system rather than periodically visiting it. Residents adapt. Tourists don't have to, because they're not staying.

When the signal is right, the system provides the amplification. When the system integrates the brand, the environment carries it forward. And when that happens, the brand has achieved something that no media budget can manufacture and no campaign timeline can contain.

It Scales Differently

—

Belonging does not scale the way influence scales, and understanding that distinction is one of the most important, and most financially uncomfortable, realizations a brand can arrive at.

The Failure of Replication

The first thing that breaks down when brands try to scale belonging using influence mechanics is replication. In influence-driven models, scaling is a matter of copying what worked and distributing it more widely. A successful campaign gets adapted for new markets, translated for new languages, and pushed through new channels. The underlying creative stays consistent because consistency is how you maintain efficiency and brand coherence across a large operation. Replication is the engine of scale.

In belonging-driven models, replication is the engine of rejection. Culture is defined by difference, by the specific, local, particular ways that communities have developed their own standards, their own signals, their own unspoken rules for what fits and what doesn't. A campaign that performs spectacularly in one cultural environment cannot simply be duplicated in another, even when the demographic data suggests the audiences are similar. The structural physics of the environments are different. The signals are different. The native behaviors are different. The internal expectations are different. What registers as a perfect fit in one space can register as an intrusive foreign object in the next, and no amount of targeting precision can compensate for that fundamental mismatch.

The Filipino birthday party illustrates this with a clarity that's hard to argue with. The format is universally recognizable, the shared food, the music, the fluid and open flow of people moving between conversations and tables. Every Filipino who has ever been to one knows what a Filipino birthday party feels like. And yet no two are identical. The energy shifts depending on the hosts. The pacing shifts depending on the crowd. The specific songs that land, the way the food is arranged, the particular rhythm of the evening, all of it adapts to the specific people and the specific space. The structure is consistent. The expression is entirely local. The system scales not by repeating itself but by fitting into each environment it enters, and the fitting is never the same twice.

The Ilocos Empanada and the Unborrowed Moment

The Ilocos empanada is having a moment right now, and the moment is entirely its own.

No rebrand. No influencer rollout. No glossy modern Filipino positioning. Just orange rice dough, egg, longganisa, grated papaya, deep fried and served hot, with a crunch that hits before you've even finished looking at it. Creators in different cities have been posting it. People are searching for it, tracking it down, driving to find it. And what's notable is that nobody is posting it to be first. They're posting it because they found something that belongs to them.

I'm part Ilocano on my father's side. I've only been to Ilocos once and I was too young to remember it. So when I started seeing the empanada spread across my feeds, I wasn't an expert reclaiming something I already knew. I was a curious descendant following a thread back to a part of my identity I'd never fully found. When I realized nobody nearby was selling them, individuals were making them out of their houses, but none close enough to reach, I decided to try making them myself. I'm still learning. That's the point.

The Ilocos empanada didn't go viral. It spread. There's a difference. Viral is manufactured, amplified, timed to a launch. Spread is organic, lateral, carried by people who recognize something before they can explain why. The momentum isn't manufactured. It's inherited, passed through the community the way food has always traveled in Filipino culture, from one person's kitchen to another, from one province to the diaspora, without anyone declaring it a trend first.

This is what belonging looks like when it scales on its own terms. Specific first. Scaled later. If at all. The community that is finding the Ilocos empanada right now isn't being reached. They're reaching back. Toward a province, toward a practice, toward a part of their identity that was always there but hasn't always been visible. Some of them, like me, are descendants who know the name of the place but not the texture of it yet. The empanada is a way in.

Culture doesn't need to be amplified to matter. It needs to be understood before you step into it.

Forensic Adaptation

Scaling belonging requires what I call *forensic adaptation*, a deep, specific understanding of each environment that allows the core principles to remain constant while the expression changes completely. The mechanics of belonging, Recognition, Participation, Contribution, Signals, Continuity, don't change from one community to the next. The framework holds. But how those mechanics are expressed, what Recognition looks like in this specific room, what Signals resonate at this particular frequency, what Contribution means to this community given its specific history and values, all of that has to be rebuilt for every new environment rather than copied from the last one.

This approach is inherently less centralized than influence-based scaling. It requires the brand to allow the work to evolve within each specific environment rather than micromanaging every expression from a single corporate headquarters. It requires local participants to have genuine influence over how the work is expressed, not as a gesture toward inclusivity but as a structural necessity, because local participants are the only people with the proximity to know what fits and what doesn't. The brand remains consistent in its core principles. The visible output varies, legitimately and intentionally, from one community to the next.

Most brand organizations are not built for this. The legal teams, the brand guidelines, the approval chains, the regional consistency requirements, all of it is designed to produce replication, not adaptation. Belonging at scale requires a willingness to build an organizational infrastructure that is genuinely capable of localized variation, which is a different problem than building a better campaign.

Trust vs. Impressions

Scaling through belonging also requires a fundamentally different relationship with time, and this is where the financial model gets genuinely difficult to defend inside most organizations.

You can buy a million impressions in a second. You cannot buy a year's worth of trust in an afternoon. Integration cannot be accelerated the way distribution can be accelerated, because trust is not a volume metric. It is a durability metric. Each environment requires its own cycle of understanding, alignment, and sustained presence before the work can truly take root. There is no shortcut that doesn't register as a shortcut. The community can feel when something is being rushed, and rushed trust is no trust at all.

But the results on the other side of that patience are far more durable than anything the influence model produces. Once alignment is genuinely established, once the community has integrated the work into its own internal life, the environment begins to support the work without requiring constant external energy to keep it moving. It breathes on its own. It continues without the brand having to drive it.

The Network of Integration

The final dimension of how belonging scales differently is the network effect it produces over time. As work integrates into multiple, overlapping cultural environments, those environments begin to connect, through the participants who move between them, sharing and extending the work into contexts the brand never planned for and may not even be aware of. Growth emerges from multiple points of integration simultaneously, rather than expanding outward from a single central campaign.

This changes what success looks like at the macro level. The relevant question stops being how many people were reached and starts being how many environments the work has genuinely integrated into, how many rooms it now lives inside, how many communities are carrying it forward without being asked to. You don't scale belonging by reaching more people. You scale it by fitting into more places, more deeply, more accurately, over more time.

Growth is not measured by the width of the broadcast. It is measured by the depth of the roots, and roots, by definition, are invisible from the outside. You know they're there because the thing keeps growing long after anyone stopped tending it.

CHAPTER 24

The Friction Of The Real

—

In the influence era, the ultimate goal of production was polish. Brands invested billions in the pursuit of flawless output, high-fidelity visuals, perfectly timed soundtracks, surgically edited narratives that left no rough edge exposed. This level of polish served a specific strategic purpose: it signaled authority. It told the audience that the entity behind the message was professional, well-resourced, and operating at a level above the ordinary. In that world, friction was a failure. Any sign of human error, any technical imperfection, any unpolished moment that let reality show through got scrubbed away to maintain the brand's distance and prestige. The smoothness was the point.

In the world we're actually living in now, that signal has inverted. We exist in an environment saturated with synthetic perfection. AI-generated imagery is anatomically flawless. AI-written copy is grammatically immaculate. The tools for manufacturing the appearance of quality have become so accessible and so powerful that perfection itself has been commoditized, and when perfection becomes a commodity, it stops being a signal of trust and starts being a signal of automation. Flawlessness is no longer the hallmark of high-tier work. It is the hallmark of the artificial. And in a world where the community has developed a near-perfect radar for what was made by a person and what was manufactured by a system, the most polished version of something is increasingly the least trusted version of it.

The Signal of Presence

This inversion has created a new standard for belonging, and it is one that most brand organizations are structurally uncomfortable with: The *Friction of the Real.*

Friction, in this context, is not a technical failure. It is the presence of human texture, the slight misalignment in a signal, the unpolished edge of a conversation, the raw and unrepeatable nature of a live interaction that couldn't have been scripted because it happened in the actual conditions of the actual world. While influence thrives on the smooth surface of a broadcast, belonging requires the tactile reality of the environment. It requires evidence that someone was actually there.

The Filipino garage party is the most precise expression of this principle I know. These spaces are defined entirely by friction, mismatched folding chairs pulled from different rooms, the hum of a portable fan doing its best against the summer heat, the unpolished acoustics of a karaoke machine that's seen better days, the specific organized chaos of too many people and too much food in a space that was never designed for either. From a production standpoint, none of this is defensible. From a belonging standpoint, every single element of it is a high-fidelity signal of home. If you replace the garage with a sterile, professionally curated venue, better lighting, better sound, no folding chairs, something essential disappears. The friction is what makes the space lived-in rather than launched. The imperfection is the proof that real people actually gather here.

Polish vs. Presence

When an environment is too polished, it stops feeling like a home and starts feeling like a set, a place that was designed to look like people live there rather than a place where people actually do. This signals something the community reads immediately: the brand is still operating as an external observer, trying to replicate a vibe from the outside rather than being a participant living within it. The polish is the tell. The flawlessness is the distance.

Friction signals proximity. It tells the community that the work was built by people, for people, within the actual conditions of the world, not in a studio designed to simulate those conditions for a camera. This is why a grainy vertical video captured in the middle of a crowd often generates more trust and more genuine participation than a million-dollar commercial. The lack of polish isn't a weakness. It is the proof of presence. It says: someone was actually here. This actually happened. I am not watching a simulation of a moment. I am watching the moment itself.

Synthetic influence is a broadcast. Belonging is a conversation with texture. And a conversation requires both parties to be present in the actual conditions of the actual world, not behind the safety of an edit.

The Wish Bus Standard

The institutional proof of this principle at scale is Wish Bus. Built by Yes The Best Productions in the Philippines, Wish Bus is exactly what it sounds like: a repurposed public bus, parked on a street, with a camera and a microphone. No studio. No sound treatment. No production budget. Artists climb on, sit down, and perform. The bus doesn't move. The camera doesn't cut away. The performance is what it is, in real time, in natural light, with whatever the street outside sounds like bleeding through.

By every measurable production standard, Wish Bus should not have become one of the most powerful music platforms in the Filipino diaspora. And yet it has over twelve million subscribers, billions of views, and a catalog of performances that have launched careers, validated artists, and created moments the community has been carrying for years. Not because the production is impressive. Because the production is absent, and the truth of the performance fills the space completely.

I remember the first time I watched Morissette Amon sing *Rise Up* on the Wish Bus. She was sitting down. No choreography, no staging, no visual spectacle of any kind. She opened her mouth and hit notes that most artists would need to stand up, build to, and reach for at the peak of a fully produced live show. She did it sitting, effortlessly, as if the song simply lived in her and she was just giving it a place to go. I got goosebumps. Not because of the production. Because there was no production, and what was left was entirely real.

That's the Wish Bus effect. Strip away everything that could be manufactured and what remains is either the thing itself or nothing. For the artists who have built their reputations there, the platform is a test of truth. The community knows it. That's why a Wish Bus performance carries a different kind of weight than a studio release or a label-backed video. It's not just a platform. It became the de facto standard for Filipino artist validation without any institution declaring it so. The culture enforced that standard on its own, the way Filipino culture enforces all its standards, through what keeps showing up and what quietly disappears.

No label built Wish Bus. No algorithm optimized it. No brand sponsored its rise. It became essential because it understood something that every overproduced campaign in this book's autopsy chapters missed: in a world saturated with synthetic perfection, the most powerful thing you can offer the community is the unedited truth of the thing itself.

The garage has twelve million subscribers. The bus doesn't move. And the whole world showed up anyway.

The Barriers of Perfection

This shift changes how the core mechanics of belonging actually operate at a practical level, and the implications run deeper than most brands realize.

Recognition is now tied to nuance and specificity rather than aspirational perfection. People no longer recognize themselves in a generic, flawless archetype. They recognize themselves in the specific, the local, and the slightly messy reality of their own lives, the thing that looks like their actual kitchen rather than a kitchen that was designed to look like their kitchen. The more perfect the image, the more it looks like it was designed for everyone, which means it resonates with no one in the way that a specific, imperfect truth resonates with exactly the right people.

Participation is actively hindered by perfection. When an environment is too polished, too complete, too finished, people are afraid to touch it. They feel like guests in a museum rather than residents in a park.

Contribution requires a work-in-progress state. If a brand arrives with a completed, flawless masterpiece, there is no room for the community to grab hold. Friction leaves those edges intentionally.

Excellence vs. Shine

None of this is an argument for low quality or careless execution. Excellence remains the baseline, the floor, not the ceiling, the minimum standard below which nothing else in this book matters. Every creative decision still needs a why, a level of craft and intention that earns the right to be in the conversation.

But excellence is now defined by the resolution of the truth, not the resolution of the pixels. It is the difference between a voice that is technically clear and a voice that is actually real. Between a campaign that was produced flawlessly and a moment that was captured honestly. Between a brand that looks like it belongs and a brand that has actually earned its place by being present in the conditions where the community lives.

For most brands, this is a genuinely difficult shift. It requires letting go of the safety of the edit, of the ability to scrub away anything that doesn't serve the narrative before anyone sees it. It requires trusting that the community will value honesty more than shine, and in most cases, they will, because they have spent years being sold shine and they know exactly what it tastes like.

THE 90-DAY BELONGING BUILD

Made Practical.
Start Here.

You don't build belonging by launching a campaign. You build it by managing how you show up over time. Most brands are not failing because they lack creativity or resources or talent. They are failing because they are managing for extraction instead of residency, optimizing for what they can take from a cultural environment rather than what they can sustainably contribute to it. Shifting from an extraction-based influence model to a residency-based belonging model is not a change in philosophy. It is a change in how time is managed, how presence is measured, and what the organization is actually trying to build. This roadmap provides the operational sequence for making that shift within a single fiscal quarter, not because belonging can be fully achieved in ninety days, but because ninety days is enough time to change direction, establish credibility, and lay the foundation for something durable.

The Observation Audit
Days 1–30

The Contribution Pilot
Days 31–60

The Continuity Framework
Days 61–90

The Observation Audit

The first thirty days are entirely about earning the right to speak by choosing to listen first. Nothing gets made. Nothing gets launched. No content goes out. The only objective is to develop a forensic understanding of the environment before attempting to enter it.

> *The community has been running without you for years. Your first job is to understand why it works, not to improve it.*

This means identifying the *Frequencies*, the patterns of behavior, language, and interaction that are already repeating within the community without any brand involvement. Not the trends. The patterns. The things that happen whether or not anyone is paying attention to them, because they are native to the environment rather than manufactured for it.

It means locating the true *Residents*, the architects of the space who command genuine trust rather than just followers. These are not necessarily the people with the largest audiences. They are the people whose presence actually shapes how the environment functions, whose absence would be noticed, whose approval means something because it is not for sale.

It means deciphering the Signal, mapping the specific language, the visual codes, the Zero Caption moments where the community connects without a translator, the shorthand that is invisible to outsiders and immediately legible to residents. This is the vocabulary of the environment, and you cannot speak it authentically until you have listened to it long enough to understand what it actually means.

The phase concludes with a Gap Analysis: a clear-eyed assessment of where the community is being underserved by the brands and institutions already present in their space. Not what the brand wants to offer, but what the community is actually reaching for that no one with a budget has bothered to provide. That gap is where the real opportunity lives, and finding it honestly is the only way to ensure that what comes next actually matters to the people it's meant to serve.

The Contribution Pilot

Once the environment is mapped, the objective shifts, but not to launching. To contributing. The goal of this phase is to add value without asking for a receipt, to put something real into the environment and let the community determine what it's worth.

> *You are not building a campaign. You are building a reputation inside a world that already has standards.*

At this stage, the work should no longer feel like a campaign. It should feel like something the community would have created on its own, whether the brand was there or not. The test is simple: if you removed the brand's name from it, would the community still want it to exist? If the answer is yes, you're building something that belongs. If the answer is no, you're still building an ad.

Instead of a traditional sponsored post or a branded activation, the question is what utility the brand can genuinely provide, infrastructure, access, or work-in-progress spaces where artists and creators can build without the brand's agenda attached. This is not about giving product. It is about providing something the environment would miss if it disappeared, something that adds to the infrastructure of the community's daily life rather than extracting visibility from it.

The 80/20 Culture Test applies here: eighty percent of the value created must be culture-first and artist-led, with only twenty percent remaining brand-visible. If those proportions are reversed, the brand is still extracting. The community will feel the imbalance before they can articulate it, and they will respond accordingly.

Critically, the pilot must be designed for the Friction of the Real. If it's too polished, too finished, too perfectly branded, the community won't touch it, because a perfect thing signals that there's no room for their contribution. You leave the edges unfinished deliberately. You create the entry points where someone can grab hold and add something of their own. The unfinished state is not a weakness. It is the invitation.

The Continuity Framework

The final thirty days are where residency either takes root or reveals itself as performance. This is the phase that requires the most from the brand organizationally, not because the creative is harder, but because it demands the one thing most corporate structures are designed to prevent: the distribution of control.

> *Belonging is not built in a moment. It is built in the return.*

Distributed Control means entrusting specific elements of the platform to the community architects, the residents identified in Phase 1, and allowing them to set the rules for that space. Control is not removed. It is reallocated to the people who already define the environment, whose judgment is more accurate than any brand guideline about what fits and what doesn't. This is not a gesture. It is a structural decision that changes who has authority in the room and what that authority is used for.

The metrics change in this phase as well. Success is no longer measured by Reach, by how many people were exposed to the brand's presence in the community. It is measured by Signal Accuracy: does the community recognize the brand as a native participant? Do the residents who were already in the room before the brand arrived treat the brand's contributions as something that belongs there? That recognition, or its absence, is the only meaningful measure of whether the work is taking root.

The phase concludes with the establishment of the Resident Charter: a clear, internal definition of how the brand shows up when there is no product launch to justify the spend, no quarterly goal to hit, no Heritage Month on the calendar. The Resident Charter is the brand's commitment to being present in the off-season, to maintaining the rhythm that belonging requires regardless of whether there is an immediate business case for doing so. The standards that brought you this far don't change in the off-season. But the presence continues independent of the campaign cycle, because that independence is precisely what transforms a guest into a resident.

When the system starts operating without you, when the community is carrying the work forward on its own, when the Culture Carriers are building inside the infrastructure you helped create, when the signal is being transmitted by the environment itself rather than the brand's media spend, you have stopped marketing and started belonging.

This is where the extraction ends. This is where the compounding equity begins. And this is where the real work, the durable work, the work that outlasts any campaign and any quarter and any individual brand manager, starts to grow roots deep enough to hold.

What This Requires

—

Belonging is not a marketing strategy. It is a different way of operating, a fundamental shift in how a brand understands its relationship to the communities it wants to be part of, and what it is actually willing to do to earn that relationship over time.

It also requires a total overhaul of how success gets evaluated. Short-term performance metrics are not irrelevant, but they are structurally incapable of capturing whether a brand has actually integrated into a culture. True integration is reflected in how the work continues to function after the campaign has ended, whether it gets carried forward by the community without the brand needing to push it, whether the Culture Carriers who were there at the beginning are still building inside the infrastructure the brand helped create, whether the signal is still being transmitted months and years after the media spend dried up. That is the metric that matters, and it requires a patience that quarterly planning cycles are not designed to reward.

This approach is inherently more complex than the one it's replacing. It requires coordination across teams that are used to operating in silos. It requires flexibility in execution that most approval processes are designed to prevent. It requires a genuine humility about the limits of what the corporate center can know and control, an acceptance that the outcome of belonging is not fully in the brand's hands, because belonging, by definition, is something the community grants rather than something the brand manufactures.

That complexity is not a flaw in the model. It is a reflection of how human environments actually operate. Culture is not static. It cannot be managed through a fixed set of actions or maintained by a single team on a consistent schedule. It evolves through interaction, and any brand that genuinely chooses to operate within it becomes part of that evolution, not as a director of it, but as a participant in it.

The role brands must move toward is not that of an external entity trying to shape behavior from the outside, but that of a genuine participant within environments that already exist and already have their own logic, their own standards, and their own very clear sense of who belongs there. This does not eliminate the need for strategy. It fundamentally changes what strategy is built around, shifting the focus from how to deliver a message to how to align with a system, how to add real value to it, and how to remain a vital and respected part of it over the long term.

The Filipino community already has a word for what this work is ultimately reaching toward. It is *Ginhawa*: the condition of total well-being, of wounds healed, of burdens lifted, of a place where no one is left behind and everyone is welcome to call it home. That is not a marketing outcome. It is a human one. And it is the only outcome worth building toward.

The brands that wait are not standing still. Every quarter spent in the influence model inside a high-context cultural environment is a quarter the community spends deciding who actually belongs there. Those decisions compound the same way belonging does, just in the wrong direction. The community doesn't leave a vacancy for the brand that eventually figures it out. It fills the space with something else, something that was willing to show up before it was convenient, and it carries that forward. By the time most brands are ready to move, the residency they were waiting to build has already been granted to someone else.

What this requires is not complicated. You start with the environment. You work with people who understand it. You design for participation. You contribute in ways that genuinely add value. And you maintain your presence long past the point where it's easy to justify internally. When the alignment is right, the system carries the work forward without needing to be pushed. The community becomes the engine. The signal transmits itself.

This is not a faster way to operate. It is a more accurate one.

And in a world defined by identity and culture, in a world where communities have the tools, the literacy, and the collective infrastructure to carry what belongs to them and reject what doesn't, accuracy is the only thing that lasts.

The 70,000

—

I've spent over thirty-five years behind the decks. I've played every kind of room, empty bars on slow Tuesday nights, small clubs where I could see every face, festivals where the crowd stretched further than the lights could reach. I've played rooms that were electric and rooms that were indifferent and everything in between. After that many years, I thought I understood what it felt like to move a crowd.

Then I watched the footage from my set at the Lapu Lapu Day Block Party in Vancouver.

I was playing "*Awitin Mo at Isasayaw Ko*" by VST and Company, a song that in most American rooms gets a warm nod of recognition, a moment of collective memory, and then the energy settles back to where it was. In Vancouver, in the middle of Canada, in front of seventy thousand people, something completely different happened. The entire crowd opened up. Not because they were told to. Not because the production cued them. Because the frequency was right, and they recognized it before they could even think about recognizing it.

I was watching the footage on a screen. I wasn't even in that moment anymore. And I found myself crying.

Not from pride, though there was some of that. Not from the scale of it, though the scale was real. I was crying because I was watching the physical proof of something I had believed for decades but had never seen demonstrated at that size, in that place, with that kind of undeniable clarity. Those seventy thousand people were not there because a brand had reached them. They were not responding to a campaign. They were not executing a call to action. They were there because they recognized a frequency, a specific, particular signal that said you belong here, this is your world, we are from the same place, and their bodies responded before their minds could catch up.

For that moment, they didn't just feel entertained.

They felt seen.

That is the difference this entire book has been trying to name. Not the difference between a good campaign and a great one. The difference between being reached and being recognized. Between attention and belonging. Between a moment that performs and a moment that lands in the body and stays there.

This is why I wrote this book, not as a framework I developed from the outside looking in, but as the record of something I have been living inside for thirty-five years, from a cousin's garage in the Bay Area to a DJ booth in Vancouver in front of seventy thousand people who sang every word back to a song that the industry said was too niche to matter.

It was never niche. It was always waiting for the right room.

Belonging isn't a metric. It isn't a moment. It is a recognition system, one that has the power to move a city and, if you're standing behind the booth when it happens, to change you completely.

Influence is an expense.

Belonging is an asset.

Trust is what gets carried.

ACKNOWLEDGMENTS

This book started as a question I couldn't stop asking: why do some communities make you feel like you belong the moment you enter, while others leave you performing membership forever?

The answer took longer than I expected and required more people than I can name.

To the Filipino artists who are doing the work without waiting for permission, who are creating from the inside out, building audiences that feel like family, and proving every day that specificity is not a limitation but the whole point. You are the living argument of this book.

To the brands that chose belonging over reach, who resisted the easier path of influence and built something their communities actually claim as their own. You made the theory real.

To the early readers who challenged the ideas before they were ready, you made the arguments stronger and caught the places where I was confusing conviction with clarity.

To the communities I observed, participated in, and learned from. You didn't optimize for belonging. You just built something real and let people find their way to it.

To my wife, who understood what I was trying to say before I had the words for it, and who built the kind of home that made writing about belonging feel like something I actually knew. And to our kids, you are the community I am most proud to be part of.

And to the reader who made it this far, belonging is not a strategy. It's a practice. Thank you for spending time with that idea.

These notes provide sources for specific data points, statistics, and attributed quotes that appear throughout the book. Firsthand observations, personal experiences, and direct conversations conducted by the author are noted as such and require no external citation.

Introduction
1. The Heritage Night boardroom story, the Panalo hat, and the author's decision to approve the final design are firsthand accounts from the author'sprofessional experience.
2. FIND, the Filipino Intercollegiate Networking Dialogue, 1999: firsthand account.
3. ISA Magazine: author's personal records.
4. Kiwi and Faith Santilla at FIND 1999: firsthand account.
5. José Rizal (1998): directed and co-produced by Marilou Diaz-Abaya, screenplay by Jun Lana, Ricky Lee, and Peter Ong Lim; Wikipedia; film records.

Part 1
Chapter 1
1. Dr. Virgilio Enriquez as originator of Kapwa philosophy: The Filipino Story Studio, "Are Filipino-Americans REALLY Filipino?" YouTube.
2. Professor Elizabeth Protacio De Castro quote ("KAPWA in English is I, you, and we together in one word") and Mahal kita linguistic example: The Filipino Story Studio, "Are Filipino-Americans REALLY Filipino?" YouTube; Professor Protacio De Castro is retired from the Department of Psychology, University of the Philippines.

Chapter 2
1. GoodPhil and Friendship Games - over seven thousand students: author's firsthand account. Friendship Games, 39th annual, 2024 - 32 organizations, approximately 2,900 attendees: Wilson, Emily. "CSUF celebrates Filipino heritage with annual competition," Daily Titan,

October 21, 2024. Friendship Games founded 1986 by PASA Kaibigan at CSUF: Daily Titan, October 21, 2024; friendshipgames.net.

Chapter 3

1. BINI Coachella 2026 Google Trends interest score of 100, second most-searched act behind Justin Bieber: Google Trends data, April 2026, reported in LionhearTV and Philstar.com, April 15, 2026.
2. BINI 21.1 million views on Coachella's official Instagram clip as of Weekend 1; Justin Bieber's clip had 22.6 million views; KATSEYE third with 14.5 million: KRON4, April 2026, citing Coachella official Instagram data.
3. BINI's Pantropiko clip subsequently surpassed 30 million views as of April 16, 2026, making BINI the most-viewed female act at the festival: Asian Journal News, April 16, 2026.
4. H.E.R. Baybayin apron as Belle - H.E.R. personally requested the addition of Baybayin script spelling "Belle" to her village outfit apron; script was hand-painted by a friend of costume designer Marina Toybina: Variety, December 2022, exclusive interview with Marina Toybina; GMA News Online, December 14, 2022; Preview.ph, December 12, 2022.

Part 2

Chapter 4

1. Jo Koy and Gabriel "Fluffy" Iglesias SoFi Stadium sellout, March 21, 2026, first-ever stand-up comedy show at SoFi Stadium, over 70,000 tickets: SoFi Stadium official press release, April 22, 2025; Variety, March 19, 2026; Art Threat, March 22, 2026.
2. Easter Sunday theatrical gross of approximately $13 million: Box Office Mojo.
3. Heavy Rotation launch with 19 artists (2007) and revival with 350+ artists (2019): author's personal records.
4. Grammy wins by artists of Filipino heritage over an eight-year stretch from 2017 through 2025: Kalani Pe'a won Best Regional Roots Music Album four times, in 2017, 2019, 2022, and 2025, for album Kuini at the 67th Grammy Awards, February 2, 2025; Pe'a is of Native Hawaiian and Filipino heritage: Inquirer USA, February 5, 2025; Grammy.com; Wikipedia. H.E.R. won Grammy Awards in 2019, 2021, and 2022. Bruno Mars won four Grammy Awards in 2022 as Silk Sonic including Record of the Year and Song of the Year. Olivia Rodrigo won three Grammy Awards

in 2022 including Best New Artist. Steve Lacy won Best Progressive R&B Album in 2023. Jesse Barrera and Jeff Bernat won Best Contemporary Christian Album as songwriters on DOE's album Heart of a Human, 67th Grammy Awards, February 2, 2025. Source: Grammy Awards official records, 2017–2025; Inquirer.net, February 6, 2025; Billboard Philippines, February 2025; MYX Global, February 13, 2025.

Chapter 5

1. Disney UK "Lola" (2020): produced by Disney EMEA's in-house creative team led by Angela Affinita, Director of Brand Marketing and Creative, in partnership with Flux Animation Studios, New Zealand. Aired in 26 countries. Source: Disney UK press release, November 9, 2020; Asian Journal News, November 10, 2020.
2. Angela Affinita quote ("Being able to draw on my own experience with my Filipina grandmother..."): The Drum, November 2020; CNN Philippines, November 20, 2020.
3. "Lola" reached 106 million views; the 2020 and 2021 films combined exceeded 184 million views: Disney UK press release, November 2, 2022.
4. "The Stepdad" (2021): Disney UK press release, November 3, 2021; Manila Bulletin, November 20, 2021.
5. Make-Your-Own Parol Lantern set: Disney UK press release, November 2, 2022.

Chapter 6

1. Friendship Games founded 1986 at California State University Fullerton by CSUF PASA Kaibigan. Largest student-run Pilipinx American event in the nation. Over 40 organizations from California, Nevada, and Arizona: friendshipgames.net.
2. GoodPhil - AJ Rafael headlining, room energy, and 20% non-Filipino attendance figure: author's firsthand account.

Part 3

Chapter 7

1. Puss in Boots: The Last Wish Oscar nomination: Academy Awards records, 95th Academy Awards, 2023.
2. Forgotten Island release date September 25, 2026, directed by Joel Crawford and Januel Mercado, cast including H.E.R., Liza Soberano,

Lea Salonga, Dolly de Leon, Jo Koy, and Manny Jacinto: DreamWorks Animation press materials.

Chapter 8

1. Eyyy origin story - Sheena Catacutan fan meet interaction with graduating fan; Sheena quote "Naiiyak ka? Eyyy ka muna, eyyy!": PhilStar Life, July 2024; ABS-CBN News.
2. Google search for BINI triggering eight Eyyy emojis as of April 2026: ABS-CBN Entertainment, April 2026.
3. Hillari won Spellemannprisen for R&B/Soul, March 2025: Spellemannprisen official results, March 2025.
4. Hillari NRK P3 Artist of the Year 2023: NRK P3 official announcement.
5. Hillari quotes ("Without my Norwegian and Filipina background...") and "I love how Filipinos show up for each other..."): Mixtape Madness interview; Joysauce.com interview.
6. Hillari Hiligaynon quote ("I will always be a proud Bagonhon..."): Good News Pilipinas, Bago City mayor's office visit coverage.
7. DJ Javier LAFC and LA Kings permanent store merchandise: direct communication with author.
8. Louis De Guzman Ma Divina x New Balance: New Balance press release.
9. Rich Tu First Generation x Nike: Nike press materials.
10. Venessa at the Filipino School of New York and New Jersey, Jason and Kat of Future Ancestors - community connectors who helped establish Hillari's network prior to her debut concert in New York: firsthand account from the author's direct involvement in connecting Hillari to the New York Filipino community network, 2025.

Chapter 9

1. EZ Mil Panalo performance: Wish Bus YouTube channel, Yes The Best Productions.
2. Bebot by the Black Eyed Peas - 2005 track written by will.i.am and apl.de.ap, rapped entirely in Filipino by apl.de.ap; went viral again on TikTok in early 2026 through a makeup transformation trend started by Filipino content creators celebrating Filipina identity: Philstar.com, "Black Eyed Peas resurface 'Bebot' videos as song trends anew," February 11, 2026; Pulp Magazine, "The 'Bebot' Effect: How a Filipino TikTok Trend Went Global," February 26, 2026; Kristina Rodulfo, "Why the Viral Filipino

'Bebot' Trend Matters," kristinarodulfo.substack.com, February 12, 2026.

3. Mundo by IV of Spades - released 2018; viral phenomenon following Wish 107.5 Bus performance; first Original Pilipino Music video in history to surpass 100 million views; debuted on Billboard Philippines Hot 100: Wish 107.5 Bus YouTube channel, youtube.com/watch?v=1P1cEEp2KpU; The Singles Jukebox, March 9, 2018; USA Inquirer, "Filipino rock band IV of Spades soars to No. 13 on US TikTok Billboard," usa.inquirer.net; Billboard Philippines, "IV of Spades 'Mundo' Debuts on the Philippines Hot 100," billboardphilippines.com.

4. Baryo Hi-Fi - co-founded by Miles Canares, Jennifer Taylor, Stephanie Ramos, Kristofferson San Pablo, and Rion Barcena; inaugural event May 4, 2024, Historic Filipinotown, Los Angeles; drew over 10,000 attendees in 2024; Nike presented "Working Overtime," a multidisciplinary art exhibit curated by Kristofferson San Pablo exploring Filipino artistry through basketball: Asian Journal, "Baryo HiFi Returns May 3 to Historic Filipinotown," April 27, 2025; myTFC, April 28, 2025; SIPA, "Baryo HiFi: A Celebration of Filipino Culture and Community," June 18, 2024.

5. Pinoys on Parliament, Ottawa - Filipino leadership conference; author's firsthand account from four years of attendance as DJ and speaker.

Chapter 10

1. Ruby Ibarra NPR Tiny Desk Contest 2025 win out of 7,500+ submissions, "Bakunawa" performed in English, Tagalog, and Bisaya: NPR Tiny Desk Contest official announcement, 2025.

2. Ruby Ibarra sold-out ten-city national tour: press coverage.

3. Sofronio Vasquez won The Voice Season 26, December 10, 2024, first Filipino and first Asian to win, coached by Michael Bublé: NBC The Voice official results; Wikipedia; Rappler, December 11, 2024; Parade, December 12, 2024; Vogue Philippines, December 2024.

4. Jessica Sanchez won America's Got Talent Season 20, September 24, 2025, while nine months pregnant, first AGT winner to compete while pregnant: NBC AGT official results; Deseret News, September 25, 2025; Extra TV, September 25, 2025; WRAL, September 25, 2025; Wikipedia.

5. Raymond Townsend - first player of Filipino heritage in NBA, 1978: NBA historical records.

6. Jordan Clarkson - grandmother Marcelina Tullao Kingsolver from Bacolor, Pampanga; NBA Sixth Man of the Year 2020-21; represented Philippines

at 2018 Asian Games and 2023 FIBA World Cup: NBA.com; FIBA official records.

7. Jalen Green - Filipino heritage through mother Bree Purganan whose grandfather is Filipino; second overall pick by Houston Rockets 2021: NBA.com; Wikipedia.

8. First two Filipino-heritage players to share NBA court, October 28, 2021, Rockets Filipino Heritage Night: Deseret News, October 28, 2021; ABS-CBN News, October 29, 2021.

9. Dylan Harper - mother Maria Pizarro born Bataan, Philippines; selected second overall by San Antonio Spurs 2025; maternal grandfather represented Philippines in jai alai at 1968 Summer Olympics: Wikipedia; Rappler, June 27, 2025; Asian Journal News, June 2025.

10. Dylan Harper quote ("My mom's side of the family, they've put so much into me."): NBA.com Philippines, June 2025.

11. Ron Harper Jr. - Filipino heritage through mother Maria Pizarro; played for Toronto Raptors on two-way contract 2022–2023; older brother of Dylan Harper: Philstar.com, July 2022; Inquirer Sports, July 2022; Wikipedia.

12. Jared McCain - traded to Oklahoma City Thunder from Philadelphia 76ers, February 2026; quote ("I am a Filipino. I mean, only like 10 percent, but that counts right?"): Inquirer.net, November 28, 2024; Wikipedia.

13. Roman Gabriel - born Roman Ildonzo Gabriel Jr., August 5, 1940, Wilmington, North Carolina; father Roman Gabriel Sr. immigrated from the Philippines; mother Irish American; second overall pick in 1962 NFL Draft by Los Angeles Rams; starting quarterback for Los Angeles Rams 1962 to 1972, Philadelphia Eagles 1973 to 1977; NFL MVP 1969, first and only Asian American to win the award; four-time Pro Bowl selection; held Rams all-time record for passing yards and touchdowns at retirement; inducted into College Football Hall of Fame 1989; played in front of one of the largest Filipino populations in America in Los Angeles; passed away April 20, 2024, age 83: AsAmNews, January 3, 2026; NBC News, April 21, 2024; PBS NewsHour, April 21, 2024; Los Angeles Rams official tribute, May 2024; Wikipedia.

14. Erik Spoelstra - mother Elisa Celino born San Pablo, Laguna, Philippines; first Asian American head coach in all four major North American sports leagues; three NBA championships with Miami Heat; head coach of Team USA: Wikipedia; GMA News; NBA Coaches Association, March 2017; Olympics.com.

15. Cam Bynum - Filipino heritage through mother Jennifer, third-generation Filipino American from San Francisco with roots in Leyte; quote ("I rep my roots heavy"): NextShark, December 2022; Indianapolis Colts official, March 2025; NFL.com.

16. Josh Jacobs - one-quarter Filipino through grandfather; father Marty Jacobs half Black, half Filipino, family roots in Angeles City, Luzon; three-time Pro Bowler, 2022 All-Pro: The Forkball, June 2025; Wikipedia.

17. Nikko Remigio - Filipino heritage through father Mark Remigio, family from Iloilo and Muntinlupa; 44-yard punt return in 2025 AFC Championship Game: Wikipedia; Rappler, April 2024.

18. Tyler Allgeier - Filipino heritage through maternal grandmother from Southern Leyte; Philippine sun and stars tattoo on upper left arm: Inquirer.net, May 2022; Wikipedia.

19. Chris Johnson - Filipino heritage through mother Priscilla Marie Mayo-Johnson; selected 27th overall by Miami Dolphins in 2026 NFL Draft: San Diego State Athletics; Wikipedia; Bleacher Report, April 2026.

20. CJ Williams - selected 203rd overall by Jacksonville Jaguars in 2026 NFL Draft: Jacksonville Jaguars official, April 2026. Community response and Cam Bynum comment ("Philippines is boomin lately"): amaznhq Instagram, April 2026; socalfilipinos Instagram, April 2026.

21. Tim Stapleton - first player of Filipino descent in NHL, debuted with Toronto Maple Leafs February 2009; half Filipino, half Irish; quote ("Someone corrected them. To this day, the joke is my friends think I called in and corrected them myself."): Wikipedia; NHL.com, November 2022.

22. Matt Dumba - Filipino Canadian defenceman; Filipino heritage through mother; seventh overall pick in 2012 NHL Draft by Minnesota Wild; co-founded Hockey Diversity Alliance; first NHL player to kneel for national anthem: Wikipedia; Canadian Filipino Net, September 2020.

23. Jason Robertson - mother Mercedes born Manila, Philippines, immigrated to US at age three; second Filipino American in NHL; first Dallas Stars player to record 100-point season: Wikipedia; Texas Monthly; NHL.com; WFAA, February 2023.

24. Nick Robertson - third Filipino American in NHL; Toronto Maple Leafs forward; younger brother of Jason Robertson: Wikipedia; USA Hockey, June 2020.

25. Filipinas FIFA Women's World Cup 2023 - 18 of 23 players US-born; Olivia McDaniel mother has roots in Pampanga and Davao, named

player of the match in 1-0 victory over New Zealand: AP/Yahoo Sports, July 2023; Rappler, July 31, 2023.

26. Hali Long quote ("Under our roof, it was purely Pinoy. That's just who I was, without question."): AP/Yahoo Sports, July 2023.

Chapter 11

1. Trader Joe's Filipino Style Chicken Adobo - product name, "Filipino Style" labeling, ingredient list including turmeric and celery seed in chicken base: Mashed.com, "The Trader Joe's Filipino-Style Food We'll Likely Never Buy Again," February 8, 2026; The Post, thepost.ph, "I tried Trader Joe's chicken adobo so you don't have to," November 27, 2025. Community response and ranking last in frozen Asian food category: Chowhound, "14 Trader Joe's Foods Customers Complain About The Most," March 29, 2026.

2. Manila Sound - emerged mid-1970s combining Filipino sounds with rock, disco, jazz, and funk; shaped by presence of US military bases and economic ties to America: IIAS Blog, "Manila Sound and the Roots of Pinoy Pop," blog.iias.asia; Wikipedia, "Manila Sound." Filipino musicians employed at US military bases across Asia, exposed to and transforming American styles into a distinctly Filipino form: Journal of Jazz Studies, Rutgers University, "Filipina Singers and Jazz in Post-Colonial Manila," jjs.libraries.rutgers.edu.

3. DJ QBert and Mix Master Mike performed at the inaugural Coachella Festival, October 10, 1999: MixesDB.com, "1999-10-10 - DJ Qbert & Mix Master Mike & Rahzel @ Coachella Festival"; Concert Archives, concertarchives.org, Coachella 1999 lineup; Setlist.fm, Coachella Festival 1999. DJ QBert (Richard Quitelvis) Filipino-American, born and raised in Daly City, California: LA Weekly, "How Filipino-American DJs Came to Dominate West Coast Turntablism," May 23, 2019. Mix Master Mike (Michael Schwartz) of Filipino and Ashkenazi Jewish descent, born and raised in the San Francisco Bay Area: Wikipedia, "Mix Master Mike."

4. apl.de.ap (Allan Pineda Lindo) - Black Eyed Peas performed at Coachella, Outdoor Theatre, April 26, 2003: The Mojave Tent, themojavetent.com, "Black Eyed Peas, Coachella 2003"; GMA News Online, "Coachella through the years: Filipino artists who rocked the festival's stage," April 13, 2026.

5. Filipino Coachella artist roster - GMA News Online, "Coachella through the years: Filipino artists who rocked the festival's stage," April 13, 2026.

6. Bruno Mars - 16 Grammy Awards from 36 nominations as of 2026, including three Record of the Year wins, Album of the Year, and Song of the Year; swept all six categories for 24K Magic at the 60th Grammy Awards in 2018: Grammy.com, "Bruno Mars Artist Page"; Wikipedia, "List of awards and nominations received by Bruno Mars."

7. BINI at Coachella 2026 - first act from the Philippines to perform at Coachella, 45-minute set at the Mojave Stage, April 10, 2026; formed through ABS-CBN's Star Hunt Academy, debuted 2020; performed "Pantropiko" and live debut of "Blush" from EP Signals: Rolling Stone, "Bini Become First Filipino Group to Perform at Coachella 2026," April 11, 2026; Hollywood Reporter, "Girl Group BINI Makes History as First Filipino Act to Perform at Coachella," April 11, 2026.

8. Paradise Rising - launched July 2020 as joint venture between 88rising and Globe Telecom; inaugural EP semilucent released July 31, 2020: Hypebeast, "88rising Announces New Philippines Sub-Label Paradise Rising," August 12, 2020; Billboard, "How 88rising Teamed With a Filipino Telco Giant to Develop Global Crossovers," September 28, 2020. Ylona Garcia, the label's most prominently signed artist, departed 2023; final semilucent EP released October 2022: NME, "Paradise Rising releases 'semilucent 3' EP," October 7, 2022.

9. Bahay kubo brand founded by Christina Nadin, Filipino-British model and influencer whose mother is Filipino with roots in Bicol; launched 2024: Rodulfo, Kristina. "Who Gets to Profit From Filipino Culture?" kristinarodulfo.substack.com, June 8, 2025.

Chapter 12

1. Ryan Cayabyab quote ("Once they play the music and start singing, it makes that community feel that they are home, that they belong. Music has that quality to make the people feel that they are at home."): The Filipino Story Studio, "The Maestro Who Wrote Your Favorite Filipino Songs," YouTube. Ryan Cayabyab is the National Artist for Music of the Philippines and Ramon Magsaysay Award recipient.

2. MYX origin - MTV agreement with Studio 23 ended; MYX launched as a music block on Studio 23, November 20, 2000; became a 24-hour channel June 2002: MYX history transcript provided to author.

3. Managing director quote ("MTV decided it really wanted to be a music

channel 24 hours a day...") and "OPM and MYX are one and the same": MYX history transcript provided to author.

4. DJ Nasty Nes Rodriguez - born in the Philippines, relocated to the United States in 1970; debuted the West Coast's first all-rap radio show Freshtracks on Seattle's KFOX 1250-AM in 1980 at age nineteen; co-founded NastyMix Records in 1985 with Sir Mix-A-Lot and Ed Locke; NastyMix released two platinum albums; hosted three rap radio shows over seventeen years; honored with Very Important Pinoy award by Filipino American National Historical Society in 1992: 206Zulu.org; FANHS Greater Seattle Chapter, October 16, 2014; Seattle Times, November 27, 2024; Humanities Washington, January 20, 2022. Quote ("I wasn't white, I wasn't Black, they didn't know what I was... one of the best gifts that God ever gave me."): Seattle Times, November 27, 2024.

5. Legaci - 34 million YouTube views for "Baby" cover, performed on Justin Bieber's My World 2.0 Tour across 30 countries: Wikipedia; East Bay Times, July 12, 2010.

6. Melissa Polinar - streams and SXSW appearance: press coverage.

7. Jeff Bernat - "Call You Mine" featured in 2014 MBC drama You Are My Destiny (Fated to Love You); led to chart success and Korean fanbase; won Grammy Award as songwriter on DOE's Heart of a Human, 2025: Korea Herald; APE Concerts; Grammy Awards official records, 2025.

8. AJ Rafael - over 1 million YouTube subscribers, founded Crazy Talented Asians: YouTube channel data.

9. Jeremy Passion - "Lemonade" has surpassed 120 million Spotify streams: Spotify, May 2026.

10. DJ E-Man - Vice President of Music and Program Director for Meruelo Media, overseeing Power 106 and 93.5 KDAY: LinkedIn, confirmed May 2026.

11. DJ Franzen career details - started as a young teen intern at KMEL, co-hosted Snoop Dogg's nationally syndicated show, became top-rated afternoon drive host in Las Vegas: DaveD.com, daveyd.com/FullArticles/articleN69.asp.

Part 4

Chapter 13

1. Jollibee first US store, 1998, Daly City, California: Jollibee Foods Corporation press materials.

2. Jollibee USA Today 10Best fast-food fried chicken award, 2024 and 2025: USA Today 10Best, August 7, 2024 and July 28, 2025.

3. Jollibee 500-store North America expansion target by 2030: Nation's Restaurant News, January 13, 2026; PR Newswire, December 23, 2025; Franchise Times, January 2026.

4. Nike terminated relationship with Manny Pacquiao within 24 hours of his comments, February 2016: press coverage, February 2016.

Chapter 14

1. Ube exports - PSA FOI request processed September 26, 2023, inquiry number PSA-792641540529, covering purple yam production data January 2017 through September 2023: foi.gov.ph.

2. Autumn Durald Arkapaw - first woman, first Black person, and first Filipina to win Oscar for Best Cinematography, for Sinners, 98th Academy Awards, March 15, 2026: Academy Awards official results; Wikipedia; ABC News, March 16, 2026; Blavity, March 16, 2026; Asian Journal News, March 17, 2026.

3. Autumn Durald Arkapaw's maternal grandfather Guillermo Pagan Bautista from Masantol, Pampanga - resistance fighter during Japanese occupation, survivor of Bataan Death March, later joined U.S. Army: Wikipedia; Vogue Philippines, March 2026; ABC News, March 16, 2026; IBTimes UK, March 16, 2026.

4. Filipino nurses statistic - nearly 30 percent of all immigrant registered nurses: Harvard International Review, October 2024 (33 percent of all foreign-born RNs as of 2022); Migration Policy Institute via Inquirer.net, June 2024 (28 percent of immigrant RN workforce). Both figures support "nearly thirty percent" as accurate.

5. The Pitt - Filipino nurse characters Princess Dela Cruz (Kristin Villanueva) and Perlah Alawi (Amielynn Abellera); Dr. Trinity Santos (Isa Briones); all three speak Tagalog on screen: Today.com; Vogue Philippines; ABS-CBN News, April 15, 2025; CBC News, 2025; GMA News, April 8, 2026; Refinery29, January 2026.

6. St. Denis Medical - Season 1, Episode 11, "Salamat You Too," aired November 26, 2024, featuring Nico Santos as Rene, veteran Filipino RN: NBC.com; Episodic Medium Substack; The Nerds of Color, November 20, 2024.

Chapter 15

1. Barkada Wine Bar, Washington D.C. - four non-Filipino owners named wine bar using the Tagalog word barkada; bar served no Filipino food or drinks; community backlash prompted name change before opening; owners issued public apology July 2020: HuffPost, "Bar Axing Name Over Cultural Appropriation, But Filipino Community Says Issue Runs Deeper," August 5, 2020; GMA News Online, "Four white guys open a resto called Barkada, get blasted for cultural appropriation," August 1, 2020; AsAmNews, July 30, 2020; Washington City Paper, July 2020.

2. Barong Tagalog colonial history - widely held account that the garment's transparent, untucked form was imposed by Spanish colonial authorities to prevent Filipinos from concealing weapons and to distinguish indios from colonizers; reclaimed as a symbol of Filipino identity and dignity: Simpol.ph, "The Barong Tagalog History: From Colonization to Canvas," January 7, 2026; Wikipedia, "Barong tagalog." Note: the colonial dress-code origin is part of the community's received cultural history; some historians note the absence of documentary records mandating the style, attributing the untucked, sheer form instead to climate adaptation and indigenous weaving tradition. The community meaning and resistance narrative are documented regardless of archival verification. Piña fiber production centered in Aklan: Grokipedia, "Barong tagalog," citing weaving practices in Kalibo, Aklan; Pineapple Industries, "Journey of the Barong Tagalog," September 29, 2020.

3. The remittance company at the next-gen Filipino concert observation and the personal account of using a remittance service to purchase a jacket from a Philippine slow-fashion designer featuring traditional Inaul weave from indigenous communities of Mindanao: firsthand account from the author's professional and personal experience.

Chapter 16

1. 2023 "Love the Philippines" tourism campaign footage controversy: Philippine Department of Tourism press statements; press coverage, 2023.

2. Coca-Cola Balikbayan Program Canada - 600 co-branded boxes distributed through nine Filipino-owned Sari-Sari stores across Greater Toronto Area, free shipping to Philippines via Atin-Ito, running for third consecutive year in 2025: Coca-Cola Canada press release, coca-cola.com/ca/en/media-centre/news/balikbayan-program-returns-2025;

LBBonline.com; Ads of the World, adsoftheworld.com/campaigns/ balikbayan-magic-hand-delivered.

Chapter 17
1. Filipino festival season calendar observation, the Ber Months personal discovery, the parol making kit tradition, and the Christmas tree in September: firsthand account from the author's personal experience.
2. Filipino-American History Month in October — the only Asian group in America with its own dedicated history month: FilAm History Month Coalition records.
3. Filipino Heritage Month in Canada recognized in June: Government of Canada official records.
4. April recognized as Filipino Food Month globally: Filipino Food Movement; FilAm History Month Coalition.
5. Paluwagan - communal rotating savings association operating in Filipino communities in the Philippines and across the diaspora: firsthand observation from the author's community experience.

Part 5
Chapter 18
1. Knorr x AJ Rafael karaoke jingle - 5.6 million views on Instagram at time of writing; AJ Rafael Instagram, collab reel with Knorr Philippines. View count subject to platform adjustments.
2. Creative direction - brand's request for an upbeat, memorable jingle; request to remove Filipino flag from video treatment; AJ Rafael's reframing toward a fun, tropical, communal tone; brand's decision to follow the artist's lead: author's firsthand account from involvement in the collaboration.

Chapter 19
1. Seafood City Late Night Madness - 76 events September through December 2025 across California, Las Vegas, Seattle, and five Canadian cities: myTFC, December 18, 2025; SF Standard, November 15, 2025.
2. Stephanie Ramos quote ("Filipino-American DJs have been quietly influencing the sound of global music for decades. Late Night Madness puts them front and center, not just as entertainment, but as cultural leaders. Seeing them control the energy of a room inside a Filipino space is powerful."): myTFC, December 18, 2025. Stephanie Ramos is Co-

Founder of Baryo Entertainment.

3. DJ JP Breganza quote ("The fact that I was able to play for four different generations of Filipinos within one room and cater to them all was so beautiful to see."): SF Standard, November 15, 2025.

4. Undiscovered SF - over $1.3 million in vendor sales; built as incubating tool for SOMA Pilipinas cultural district in San Francisco: SOMA Pilipinas.

Chapter 20

1. Festival of Philippine Arts and Culture, FPAC, Southern California: FPAC official records; firsthand observation from the author's community experience.

2. The Institutional Pattern observation - brands arriving late to communities after residency is established: firsthand account from the author's professional experience across multiple brand engagements.

Part 6

Chapter 21

1. Jollibee first US store opened in 1998 in Daly City, California: Jollibee Foods Corporation press records; Wikipedia.

2. Jollibee named number one fast-food fried chicken in America, USA Today 10Best award 2024 and 2025, beating Chick-fil-A, Popeyes, and KFC: USA Today 10Best, 2024 and 2025.

3. Jollibee plans to expand to 500 stores in North America by 2030: Jollibee Foods Corporation investor relations; press coverage.

4. Illa Manila, Kampeon, Sunkissed Pinay, Monday Suck, Abakada, Bago, Isla Project, Abaka, Sago Studio, Nostalgia - Filipino-American independent brands: direct observation; brand websites.

5. Taglish as behavioral identity marker and code-switching between Tagalog and English: firsthand observation from the author's community experience.

Chapter 22

1. Royal Caribbean Washy Washy before Yummy Yummy - Filipino crew members turning hand-washing instruction into communal performance: firsthand observation by the author during travel.

2. Filipino potluck culture and the unwritten standard of what gets brought to the table: firsthand observation from the author's community experience.

3. Integration and Autonomy framework: author's original framework developed through professional practice.

Chapter 23

1. Ilocos empanada - orange rice dough, egg, longganisa, grated papaya, deep fried: firsthand observation and personal culinary research by the author.
2. The author is part Ilocano on his father's side: firsthand account.
3. Forensic Adaptation framework: author's original framework developed through professional practice.
4. Filipino birthday party observation - structure consistent, expression entirely local: firsthand observation from the author's community experience.

Chapter 24

1. Wish Bus - over 12 million subscribers; built by Yes The Best Productions, Philippines: YouTube channel data, May 2026.
2. Morissette Amon Rise Up performance: Wish Bus YouTube channel, Yes The Best Productions.

Interlude: Bayanihan 2.0

1. Balangay boats as Austronesian origin of the word barangay; community-first architecture of early Filipino seafaring culture; every person contributing to the voyage as the founding logic of communal life: The Filipino Story Studio, "What It Truly Means To Be Filipino," YouTube; "Why Filipinos Value Family and Community So Deeply," YouTube. Austronesian migration to the Philippine archipelago dated to approximately 4,000 to 5,000 years ago, with migration out of South China to Luzon believed to predate 5000 BC: Sinaunangpanahon.com, "The Complex and Diverse Pre-Colonial Philippines Before Spanish Arrival," April 28, 2025; Science and Engineering Journal, "The Kalaga Putuan Crescent and the Austronesian," 2024, vol. 17, no. 1. Oldest known balangay boats carbon-dated 689 to 988 CE, recovered from Butuan, Agusan del Norte: Wikipedia, "Balangay."

Closing

1. Ginhawa defined as the Filipino concept of total well-being, freedom from burden, a place where no one is left behind and everyone is welcome

to call it home: The Filipino Story Studio, "The Hidden Meaning of Ginhawa Every Filipino Must Know," YouTube.

Coda
1. Lapu Lapu Day Block Party Vancouver 2024 - inaugural event, April 27, 2024, organized by Filipino BC and Sunset on Fraser Business Association: Philippine Consulate General Vancouver, April 30, 2024; Global News, April 28, 2024.
2. Attendance figure of seventy thousand: author's firsthand account.
3. The author DJed at the 2024 event: firsthand account.

Marlino Bitanga is the founder and CEO of Makeeta, a culture-led creative and production partner that builds real relationships between brands and Next-Gen Filipino culture. Known in the music world as DJ Marlino, he has spent over three decades navigating the space between corporate structures and the underground, from a cousin's garage in the Bay Area to boardrooms, festival stages, and conference halls across the US, Canada, and the UK.

He is the creator of Heavy Rotation, the first and largest platform dedicated exclusively to Filipino Hip-Hop and R&B, built not because the industry asked for it but because the gap was too large to ignore.

For thirty-five years, Marlino has operated on a single frequency. This book is what that frequency sounds like when you write it down.

Based in Southern California.

If the principles in this book resonated, but the execution feels out of reach, it is likely because your organization is still running on a broadcast model in a belonging world.

Makeeta works with brands that are ready to stop being tourists. We guide how organizations show up authentically in Next-Gen Filipino culture, develop artists as genuine creative partners, and produce the work that proves those relationships are real rather than performed. We specialize in the high-context environments where generic influence fails, where the difference between a moment and something that lasts is whether the community actually recognizes you as one of theirs.

The frequency exists. We help you find it.

www.makeeta.co

www.ingramcontent.com/pod-product-compliance
Lightning Source LLC
Chambersburg PA
CBHW031143160726
47991CB00004B/1546